Praise for *Succ*

Success Curious is more than just a guide to high performance – it's an inspiring testament to overcoming obstacles. Andy Reid's journey, marked by challenges and labels that could have held him back, adds a powerful dimension to his insights on influence, connection and happiness. Through engaging stories and practical tools, Andy invites readers to not only dream bigger but to redefine what's possible in their lives. This book proves that, no matter the odds, true success is within reach for anyone willing to pursue it.

Rik Rushton
Communication Coach, author, TEDx speaker

Success is something that plenty want but few achieve. This book will help more people to discover not only what success means to them but also how they can bring it into their lives with strategies that make sense. Andy's humour and humility make it very easy to consume, and he actually explains a lot of the commonly-known elements to success in a way that will allow many people to finally take action.

Dan White
Chief Executive, Ray White

SUCCESS CURIOUS

HOW TO DEFINE AND ACHIEVE HIGH PERFORMANCE

ANDY REID

MAJOR
STREET

SUCCESS CURIOUS

ANDY REID

MAJOR
STREET

To Eliza, who saved me.
To Cal, who made me.

All my love,
Dad

About the author

Andy Reid is a coach, mentor and sought-after public speaker. In 2022, he was recognised as Australian Auctioneer of the Year. Outside of his professional life, he has a huge focus on community engagement: he has helped raise more than $3 million for charities and community groups since 2015. Always curious about success, Andy is the host of the popular *High Performance Humans* podcast, which provides him with a platform to interview many other high achievers and help to make success feel more accessible. An advocate of mental health, Andy is an ambassador for mental health charities and initiatives, calling on his own challenges in the space and giving talks to empower others to take action. Originally from the UK, Andy now lives on the Mornington Peninsula, Victoria. *Success Curious* is his first book.

To connect with Andy, please scan the QR code.

MAJOR STREET

First published in 2025 by Major Street Publishing Pty Ltd
info@majorstreet.com.au | majorstreet.com.au

© Andy Reid 2025
The moral rights of the author have been asserted.

A catalogue record for this book is available
from the National Library of Australia

Printed book ISBN: 978-1-923186-13-2
Ebook ISBN: 978-1-923186-14-9

Cover design by Typography Studio
Internal design by Production Works

10 9 8 7 6 5 4 3 2 1

Contents

Introduction

When you think of the word 'success', what comes to mind? Can you conjure up an image that represents success to you right now? Is it a fast car, nice clothes and luxury holidays with a tanned significant other? Is it having time with your friends, family and loved ones? Does it have something to do with a particular career goal, or is it something else entirely?

Success is a complex concept and means something different (even if just slightly) to every person on the planet, making it hard to find advice that perfectly fits your vision. We chase success, believing it will bring us happiness, yet we often struggle along the way. Buzzwords like 'sacrifice', 'discipline' and 'consistency' are thrown at us like salt on hot chips via inspirational quotes that have undoubtedly been plagiarised and doctored from some poor Stoic back in ancient Greece.

The harsh truth is that not many of us get to see our vision of success in real life – and that's a bit shit!

The barriers to success

Whether it's due to your upbringing, past or present circumstances, current financial reality or whatever else, you may feel limited in your capabilities while watching various Instagram

Reels of the rich and famous as they swan through life seemingly in a bubble that protects them from troubles and challenges.

Aside from that, the sheer volume of noise in the world is bloody mental! Everyone's protesting about something, obnoxious people are being really fucking loud, and there are a million versions of those bullshit get-rich-quick schemes and even more opinions on how you should be running your life in some way, shape or form!

There are so many distractions and excuses for not making more from your life, and when you get to a certain age and throw in life's 'standard' responsibilities like family and children, it's no real surprise to find yourself stuck in a life that has you thinking, 'I could do so much more', with a distinct lack of contentment, if not resentment, for the choices that you have or haven't made to this point.

Let's get curious...

I wrote this book to simplify the journey towards your version of success, making it more attainable by bridging the gap between commonly known solutions and your current reality. The book also aligns with my podcast, *High Performance Humans*, in which I interview lots of successful people from different disciplines and walks of life to uncover relatable elements and inspire you to ask, *Well, if they can do it, why can't I?*

This is where we hit a sticking point, and it's the question this book aims to address: if we know what it takes to be successful, see it constantly on social media, listen to all the audiobooks about it and hear motivational speakers like Tony Robbins talk about it constantly, then why aren't we doing the stuff that we need to do?

It's unlikely that we don't want success. Even the most cynical or unenthusiastic people would appreciate the chance to relax a bit more! So, if we want some level of success and understand the steps needed to attain it (or at least the concepts behind them), there must be a gap we haven't yet identified on an individual level.

You can argue, 'If it was easy, everyone would do it', or, 'Some people just aren't cut out for success', but these are throwaway lines that define the way society has become judgemental to the point that lots of people simply accept they can't go and get it. Alternatively, we might be hesitant to forge our own identity and path to success because of the various causes, campaigns and protests going on that have created so much noise in our world and brains.

Well, fuck that. Everyone needs a little bit of success in their lives, and everyone was born to be great. (It's the surrounding conditions that have created limitations in our minds.) You just need to work out how you can bring that to life for yourself.

The plan of attack

Understanding the gap in our approach to success isn't about placing blame; the gap is simply a reflection of how life and society have evolved without giving us time to question the status quo. To address this, I've put together a whole bunch of questions that most of us think about when we hit barriers or limitations in our thinking around what success looks like, and then brought in knowledge from my podcast guests alongside evidence from a load of research papers and studies that I had way more fun reading than I care to admit.

I've divided the book into four parts: Success, Influence, Connection and Happiness. I take a deeper-than-normal dive into the topic of success, because most of these books and online programs don't give you a depth of understanding that allows you to connect success to your life. I then look at how you can better influence yourself and those around you without backstepping.

From there, I focus on how you can build better connections within your version of success so that you can anchor yourself to a better life in today's world. Finally, I discuss how you can make sure that you're happy doing what you do, because there's no point chasing success if you're going to be miserable doing it!

There's some straight shooting in the following pages, because let's face it, a number of our excuses for our lack of success are rubbish. Hopefully, this book brings a new perspective that allows you to finally get past the excuses and onto a better path for your life.

All being well, by the end of the book we'll have worked together to break some old chains that have held you down to this point, quietened down all that noise in your head and helped you define a purpose, identity and route to success that will give you the contentment you've been trying to find.

What got you to this point?

To understand where you are now and where you'd like to go, it's important to reflect on where you've come from and assess the current state of things. This means being honest with yourself, facing any challenges and acknowledging what you're doing well.

Start by grabbing a new journal or notebook and titling it 'My success curious'. (To be fair, the title's not important; call it 'Darren' or 'Diana' if you want, as long as you know what it's for!) As you read, note down or highlight your biggest takeaways from the book.

Take some time now to sit quietly and answer the following questions in as much detail as possible:

- On a scale from one to ten, how successful do you feel your life has been to this point?

- Which areas of your life have been successful? Why?

- Where do you feel like you have let yourself down? Why?

- Have you ever been on a roll (in 'flow state')? What were you doing at the time? What was happening around you?

- What repetitive behaviours do you have that you inherently know aren't great for you (bad habits)?

- Have you ever set goals? How many of them did you achieve? Why didn't you achieve any that weren't reached?

- What values do you have? Do they genuinely sum you up, or are they just values you think you should have?

- What barriers are really holding you back? Which represent genuine compromises (such as children) and which are self-imposed?

- How much regular exercise do you partake in?

- What skills, attributes and behaviours do you have that you enjoy and are confident will be useful moving forward? Which have been missing?

After you've answered these questions, take some time to review your responses and reflect on them. Can you add more details or adjust your answers based on your reflection? This process might be a bit challenging, but as many recovery groups say, improvement begins with acknowledging the truth. Becoming aware of both your strengths and weaknesses helps you move forward with a clearer perspective.

When you finish the book, take some time to review your answers and see if any of your perspectives have shifted. You might also note any new ideas for changes you want to make in your life. Now that you have a clearer understanding of where you stand, certain parts of the book may resonate with you more than others, depending on the areas where you feel you need the most growth. That's perfectly OK. Allow what resonates to take root and revisit the other parts whenever you're ready.

PART I

SUCCESS

efore we begin this search for 'success', it might be a good idea to work out what it is in the first place! The last thing I want this book to do is give you a platform for success that's not built on a solid foundation of understanding. Many get-rich-quick schemes you see pushed around social media are built on wobbly structures that are sold on the premise that they'll work 'quickly' but very rarely result in tangible success. I've tried to shortcut plenty of things in my life, and the inevitable correlation between each attempt is a distinct lack of achievement or sustainability in the long term, so balls to that!

I'm not saying that you can't feel a sense of success in your life in a relatively short period of time, but instead of settling for a short-term bandaid, let's build a knowledge and awareness base that makes a permanent improvement you can rely on forever.

Questions we'll explore in this part of the book

- How do we define success?
- Is setting goals the path to your success?
- How can you stay motivated?
- What else impacts success?

Chapter 1

How do we define success?

I've failed over and over and over again in my life.
And that is why I succeed.

Michael Jordan

Have you ever struggled to define success for yourself? I know I have, and it frustrates me to no end. There are so many cliches around it, too. It's enough to make you want to vomit in a sea of pseudo-Hollywood motivational videos!

When it feels as if it's getting thrown in your face constantly, you can become somewhat obsessed or even depressed by the notion of success. I got stuck in this endless pursuit, always feeling as if I needed to achieve more achievements to be considered successful, no matter what I actually accomplished. It's very annoying.

That flicker of something that resembles success can be so fleeting you miss it before you've had a chance to savour it. In today's fast-paced world, by the time you reach a personal summit, you'll see that four other people on your Instagram feed have gone that little bit further than you. You can't help but make that comparison that casts a shadow over your own accomplishments. Perspective and perception heavily influence this frustration, creating both an internal and external battle.

For me, a vivid example of this occurred the day I was given the tremendous honour of conducting one of the country's biggest public charity auctions: the televised Good Friday Appeal. I had to auction off a brand-new house that had been built and donated to The Royal Children's Hospital. The cameras were on, the crowd was cheering and it was time to rock and roll. We raised $903,000 for the charity in the space of around 12 minutes. This was a record at the time and the organisers, the crowd and the charity were absolutely overjoyed. Lots of praise flowed my way, as well as smiles and pats on the back.

How did I feel, though? I felt disappointed, dejected and, to be honest, more than a little bit pissed off. I had set my definition of 'success' for this auction at $1 million. By falling short I left the auction riddled with guilt that I hadn't been a success (in my mind) for the charity.

Now, I can hear you saying, 'Come on, get over yourself. That's a great effort!' It highlights exactly why success is almost impossible to define. Although the outcome was great looking at it from the outside, it was all about the standard that I had set for myself. What other people thought at that moment didn't matter much to me because it didn't meet my own expectations.

Surely, you've encountered this situation yourself on one or more occasions: you achieve a certain threshold moment or mark in your life, such as passing an exam, winning silver in a competition or playing an instrument in a concert, and yet when people congratulate you it feels false or almost patronising, to the point that you start to feel anxious.

'Success' is a word that gets thrown around more than a dog's tennis ball, and a lot of the time it feels just as slobbery when it's delivered back to you! So, how can we define success in a way that affords us the chance to feel good about it? How can we create the headspace required to savour each moment in singularity?

Later in Part I, I'll go into the mechanics and emotions of capturing success and registering how it feels. For now, let's put a bit of thought into how success has been defined in the past so we can formulate our own definition and thus make success feel tangible. I don't know about you, but I still struggle with this from time to time. It has a lot to do with losing sight of what success means to me, which is a slippery slope towards being somewhat fucked regardless of the heights one achieves! So, let's ground ourselves in understanding the origins and evolutions of success.

How has success been defined over time?

This may make me sound like a massive geek, but it's bloody interesting to dig into different eras to see how success has been defined and revered.

The *Cambridge Dictionary* definition of 'success' has the rather subjective and ambiguous word 'positive' in it: 'The achieving of desired results, or someone or something that achieves positive results.' *The Oxford English Dictionary* is a little more succinct because it focuses on a single point in time, defining success as 'the achievement of a goal'.

If we head back to the word's Latin roots (I warned you, huge geek at heart!), we get a clue or two that can help us. The origin of the word 'success' is *succedere*, which means 'to come close after'. From there it became *successus*, which means 'advance'. The implication here is that success is progress; that is, to succeed is to advance from the position we are in.

The historical definition of success is almost unrecognisable from the popular interpretation today. The ancient Greek philosopher Aristotle believed that success was connected to being 'completely in service to society', which is consistent with his beliefs around the pursuit of material goods. His work *The Nicomachean Ethics* focuses on the pursuit of the highest form of 'good' or 'happiness', the term for which is 'eudemonia'. Aristotle despised the notion that material goals provide any real measure of 'human' success, deducing that the end products in the pursuit of success vary depending on the situation:

> *Now, as there are many actions, arts and sciences, their ends also are many; the end of the medical art is health, that of shipbuilding a vessel, that of strategy victory, that of economics wealth. But where arts fall under a single capacity … in all of these the ends of the master arts are to be preferred to all the subordinate ends; for it is for the sake of the former that the latter are pursued.*

In a practical sense, what Aristotle refers to as the 'chief good' is the knowledge you gain along the way, rather than the end product. For example, an artist doesn't learn how to paint so that they can have lots of pictures to hang, but to become an artist; and you don't (or shouldn't) get your first aid certificate for the bit of paper at the end, but to be able to help people in need:

> *Will not the knowledge of it, then, have a great influence on life? Shall we not, like archers who have a mark to aim at, be more likely to hit upon what is right?*

Plato, another Greek philosopher (pre-Aristotle), thought along similar lines, determining success by how you engage in action with wisdom and intelligence, as opposed to the completion of said action. Across the board, the philosophical godfathers all saw the growth of wisdom, knowledge or intelligence as the true North Star of success.

If we look elsewhere we find variations of the theme. For instance, you can look at any religion and quickly discover that it's not about what faith brings you, it's about maintaining faith along the journey of life. For example, the Bible has many references to the growth of one's faith being the golden ticket for success in life:

Commit to the Lord whatever you do, and he will establish your plans. (Proverbs 16:3)

Take delight in the Lord, and he will give you the desires of your heart. (Psalms 37:4)

There are also plenty of examples that take a swipe at the pursuit of material things and using the material world as the barometer for success:

What good is it for someone to gain the whole world, yet forfeit his soul? (Mark 8:36)

In Buddhism, there's a huge focus on the impermanence of life and on attachment leading to the downfall of your happiness.

Even as the world progressed from prominently religious beliefs to a greater focus on economic beliefs as modern societal structures formed, there remained a focus on self-enrichment rather than on the outcome. The ancient Romans, who one could argue pioneered modern-day 'class' systems, still underpinned their success with their lifelong devotion to the gods. One of the most prominent figures of the Industrial Revolution, James Watt, was an advocate for the brilliance of the individual as opposed to fitting in to please, and was attributed for saying: 'Don't waste your time trying to fit in. Stand out, and let people fit in with you.' Since then, an understanding that short-term material wins rarely lead to long-term happiness was maintained by industrial and capitalist leaders, such as Henry Ford: 'The short successes that can be gained in a brief time and without difficulty are not worth much.'

The myth of overnight success

Have you ever heard this phrase (or a variation of it): 'It's taken me 15 years to become an overnight success'? You hear it all the time from business success stories and sports stars who are constantly talking about their processes and commitment.

One of the most common themes in my podcast interviews has been the need for consistency and to be in love with the process or, as some put it, a hunger to continue in their growth. I ask every guest what their definition of a 'high performance human' is to see how they define success (leaving it ambiguous intentionally to see where their minds go), and some of the answers give tremendous clarity within a sentence:

Someone who has achieved a lot ... but yet is restless for what is possible. (Dan White, Chief Executive, Ray White Group)

High performance is about consistency over intensity ... anyone can go to the gym for a week, but when you look at it over an extended period of time, I think consistency is key to high performance. (Hannah Gill, Director, The Property Collective)

I think discipline is a big one ... patience ... Being on a journey where it's just the unknown (a.k.a. life), I've had to diversify my skill set, being flexible, and malleable, and jumping on opportunities when they come. (Danielle Weber, artist)

Keep turning up, no matter what. (Francesca Dean, cerebral palsy advocate)

History is full of examples demonstrating that success may not be defined by the goal but rather the progress made, both within and externally, to reach the goal. Understanding this will help us when we talk about chasing satisfaction in our lives later in Part I. What I can safely say is that a goal can't be the bullet-point definition of success – meaning the flashy car does not automatically brand you as successful, but the growth that you had to achieve in order to make the car financially viable most certainly could be classed as success.

Myths around success

It's easy to get confused by the many different variations of how success is represented in life and on social media feeds, and to worry about which is genuinely worth pursuing. A lot of articles and papers have been written about this. There are a few very common misconceptions (or myths) around success that are worth highlighting:

- **Myth – Success is measured by your bank account.**
  This myth may impact mental health in a couple of ways, as studies conducted by the American Psychological Association found that 72% of adults studied are stressed due to money-related concerns.

- **Myth – You have to make your passion your career.**
  As much as we acknowledge that money does not necessarily equal success, it does make the world go around! Some passions can most certainly be turned into incredibly fulfilling careers, but some are destined to be hobbies due to a lack of skill or a market for said talents – and that's OK too!

- **Myth – Sacrifice is a necessity.**
  This merciless identity of success that is pushed pre-
  dominantly by alpha personalities can lead to success
  in one singular part of your life but can often lead to
  immense unhappiness elsewhere. Michael Phelps, the
  most decorated Olympian in history, has spoken about his
  desperate bouts of depression that were brought about by
  only seeing himself as a swimmer and not a human, because
  of his complete sacrifice of everything in his pursuit of
  swimming perfection.

- **Myth – Working all hours is a required payment.**
  This is my personal favourite. We have this guilt that if
  we're not working, we're falling behind, but data alone
  proves that this is a hugely misguided notion. In 2024, a
  report titled *Fatigue and fatigue research: The Australian
  experience* estimated that fatigue had cost Australian
  businesses AU$5 billion in productivity annually. A strong
  work ethic is absolutely a key ingredient in sustainable
  success, but so is having enough energy to remain
  consistent in our actions!

- **Myth – Fake it until you make it.**
  With the volume of information out there, do you honestly
  think that anyone can fake that much these days? Ironically,
  despite many of us knowing this to be the case and even
  calling it out, we still get sucked into the narrative on social
  media because of social media's unrelenting 'highlight
  reel' nature.

There are a few other myths that I'm sure you will have heard
being yelped during some rabble-rousing speech or in one
of those motivational YouTube videos, but when we study

humanity's relationship with success, it becomes quite clear that success is found in the growth achieved by humans in their pursuit of a temporary goal.

Can you be successful without failing?

As we venture forth in search of progress, we tend to encounter potholes and pitfalls that can test our resolve, make us stumble and lead us to doubt our path (or even cease to continue).

To define success, we need to balance the conversation by also talking about failure and the part that it plays in our voyage towards a successful horizon. This is the bit that most of us get stuck on, because who on earth likes to fail? Unfortunately, failure is something that we cannot avoid in life.

When it comes to modern-day vernacular around the relationship between success and failure, I've got to be honest and say that some of it is rather wanky! However, as with many things, knowledge is power, so before we draw conclusions, let's dig into the perceptions around failure so we've got clarity on both sides of the fence.

Historically speaking...

Failure has often been viewed not entirely negatively, as long as it is anticipated and framed appropriately in advance. Historically, Stoics were in unison in believing that as long as we are prepared for all outcomes, then any outcome can be seen as an advancement from the position where we began. The ancient Greek philosopher Seneca said, 'Nothing happens to the wise man contrary to his expectation', and Roman Emperor Marcus Aurelius said, 'The impediment to action advances action. What stands in the way becomes the way'.

As industry took over, failure was embraced by inventors, scientists and entrepreneurs as a step required to gain enough knowledge to succeed. Albert Einstein is said to have described failure as 'success in progress', and Thomas Edison is believed to have said, 'I have not failed 700 times. I have not failed once. I have succeeded in proving that those 700 ways will not work. When I have eliminated the ways that will not work, I will find the way that will work'.

Even in sports, failure is seen as a part of the journey towards success rather than diametrically opposed to success. In fact, elite athletes often talk fondly of their failures:

I've missed more than 9000 shots in my career. I've lost almost 300 games. Twenty-six times, I've been trusted to take the game-winning shot and missed. I've failed over and over and over again in my life. And that is why I succeed. (Michael Jordan)

In tennis, perfection is impossible. In the 1526 singles matches I played in my career, I won almost 80% of those matches. Now ... what percentage of the points do you think I won in those matches? Only 54% ... when you lose every second point on average, you learn not to dwell on every shot. (Roger Federer)

So, instead of failure being something that we should fear or avoid, what becomes obvious when we look at those who have become successful is that failure is not only inevitable but in fact necessary if we are to discover the success that we set out for in the first place.

Taking it a step further, you could argue that true failure only occurs when you give up entirely on pursuing a particular goal. As many thought leaders suggest, not learning from a setback on the path to success could be considered the real failure.

Modern-day commentary around failure

If we agree that failure is necessary, does that mean we should become comfortable with it?

In the ra-ra pump-ups that I'm sure you will have seen or heard, people say things like, 'I eat rejection for breakfast!' and 'I love to fail because it gets me closer to success!' They're normally said by loud people in sponsored Instagram posts, with their chests pumped out and a weird 'ding' sound whenever they crack a smile while they sell you some sales course or measure their appendages while basking in their own magnificence.

Do you really think that any of the people I've just quoted were happy to fail? When Edison flicked on the 207th light bulb, do you think that he stood there saying, 'Man, I hope this one fails too!' and then celebrated when it popped and broke? And if you watch any of the 26 game-winning shots that Michael Jordan missed, he wasn't exactly bursting with pride or skipping off the court!

If you have any genuine ambition to have success in your life, then this modern narrative that suggests if we want to be successful then we need to be 'happy' in failure is absolute bollocks! Failing is supposed to be a lesson, not a reason to be smiling in the realisation that we didn't get it right! If we're happy in failure, then we wouldn't have the drive to pursue something better, right?

Our brains are programmed a lot more by mistakes than success. Back in the caveman days, all our brains did was protect us from harm, so since day one it has been wired as a safety defence mechanism. A study by Elizabeth Kensinger in 2009 in the US has shown that we process bad memories more than good ones, making them easier to remember. The reason for that is our senses tend to become heightened and thus register and process a lot more information when we are 'in danger' (when something bad is happening). So, if you really want to learn from your mistakes or failures and remember those lessons, then it is better for you in the long term to allow those failures to sting a bit. Allow that pain to register so your recall of the event becomes a memory that will serve you well in the future.

On top of that, in my experience it's better to accept what is, rather than fake some bullshit that isn't, and being frustrated by a failure is rather appropriate while attempting to achieve any level of success. Denying yourself certain feelings because society deems them 'weak' or 'wrong' only leads you to harbour the ill feelings for longer. The sooner you are happy to accept that failure is shit, you're way more likely to drop your ego, learn something from the failure and advance yourself closer to what you're going for. I mean, come on, who in their right mind ever starts something with the aim to fail miserably?

If we accept that failure is part of the success journey, and we're aware that it's going to sting initially but the lesson will be worth it, then we'll need another ingredient to make sure that we can get over these failures and keep moving forward: i.e. a personal definition of success.

How do we define success for ourselves?

Now that we have a much better grasp on both success and failure, it's a good idea to set a few parameters around what success looks like to you so that, as you go through the rest of the book, you can build on it with the stuff we'll go through together.

Some or all of these parameters – or guiding principles, you might say – will likely challenge you both superficially and on a deeper level. An unfortunate thing I've discovered about success is that the majority of society isn't that keen on you becoming overly successful, so if you have conformed to societal norms (consciously or unconsciously) then at least some of these parameters will be foreign to you.

Why's that? Basically, to be successful, you have to operate above the standard way of being, which is what most people tend to stick to. It's not like this book is about making you better than other people, because this is about **you** and no one else, but the problem is that becoming a better version of yourself will obviously change you in some way, and people generally don't like change!

Here's a process that may seem a bit airy-fairy, but give it a chance – I'll set some parameters that might make it feel more practical. I felt awkward the first time I did it, but there are tangible benefits to getting past that awkwardness.

You're going to need a pad, a pen and a solid hour or so in a space that allows your mind to relax. For some people that may be out in a park or amongst nature; for others it might be a bustling cafe; or it could be with your bare arse on the bottom of a hot bathtub. Wherever it is, give yourself permission to be free from concern for a short time.

Put your phone onto 'emergency calls only' (because turning it off may be a step too far if you have kids or other dependants in your life), and before you get into it give yourself five to ten minutes to acclimatise to the environment.

Ask yourself: What would my ideal life look like, feel like, sound like and be like in my current world?

Say it aloud. Repeat it a few times. Close your eyes, take a couple of deep breaths, then breathe normally.

Start to form a picture in your mind of what you ideally want your life to look like within the context of your world. What I mean by that is, if your picture involves you wearing a red cape and flying into burning buildings to save the damsel in distress, you're not exactly visualising in the context of your world!

Once you start to see a picture in your mind, define as much detail as you possibly can and write it all down. For example, when I first did this, I pictured myself driving up to my house after work. I could describe the feeling of the steering wheel of the car I wanted to drive. I could tell you the type of driveway I had, the colour of the bricks, and the sound of kids and dogs clattering down the hallway as I opened the door. I could even tell you the time that the clock on the wall had on it!

Keep writing as much as you can, and don't force yourself to write stuff because you feel you should. If it's not flowing out of you, it doesn't belong on the page.

Once you come to a natural end, relax and read back to yourself what you've written out loud. If it makes you smile and potentially gives you goosebumps, then you have an image of what success means to you.

From here, we'll look at reverse-engineering some goals and targets, but we first need to set some parameters that will help us to bring this image of success to life. Now, because I'm a fan of simplicity, we're only going to set a few agreements that will help you to build, grow, protect and gain support for your pursuit towards success. However, only having a few does mean that they are bloody important and cannot be compromised on – so no excuses!

1. Be transparent with your loved ones

Let's be tremendously clear about one thing (and I will keep saying this to you for a reason): **your definition of success is totally unique to you**. There are no opinions, political movements, TikTok trends or immediate relatives (including your parents!) that get a say in what your definition of success is or evolves into.

However, as with all things, at some point you're going to need a bit of support from time to time if you hit a hurdle or just can't be bothered – you're going to need some accountability. Not only that, but you will also want to make this process as resistance-free as possible, and if your loved ones are a part of this image you have for success then they kind of need to know about it!

People who care about you want to see you do well, but if they don't understand at least what you're wanting to achieve then they will struggle to compute any changes you go through to get there. The people you care about and value the opinions of need to be given the courtesy of being told what is going to be important to you in this journey towards success; otherwise, they may well reject the notion once you've set off on the journey.

2. Set protective boundaries around your internal fire

It sounds a bit dramatic, but I think you might know what I'm alluding to. This detailed image that you have will come under attack at various stages, both internally and externally, be it from other opinions, peer pressure, your own lethargy, or temptation. You need to give yourself permission to stay on your path towards success and not feel bad about stopping people who want to take you away from your path.

3. Understand and accept the cost of entry

The quicker you realise that the cost of entry is time and effort, the closer you'll get to whatever you deem as success. There are a few elements that contribute to the collective amount of effort required, including discipline, consistency and sacrifice of certain things that may be tempting in the short term.

Our ability to resist immediate gratification in favour of a greater long-term reward has been extensively studied due to its significance in achieving a better life. One of the most well-known experiments in this area is the marshmallow test, conducted by Walter Mischel, Ph.D. In this study, preschoolers were placed in a room individually with a single marshmallow for about

15 minutes. Mischel told each child that if they could resist the temptation to eat the marshmallow until he returned, they would receive two marshmallows. The study found that the children who were able to wait became adults who were more likely to earn higher incomes and less likely to become overweight.

Another notable long-term study, conducted in New Zealand by Terrie Moffitt, Ph.D, and her team, tracked 1000 individuals from birth to the age of 32. The study found that children who demonstrated strong willpower grew up to become adults with better mental and physical health, fewer substance-abuse issues and healthier financial habits. I bet they didn't have a marshmallow addiction, either!

Here's something I've noticed about discipline: it just doesn't stick if you don't truly desire the outcome or have strong reasons backing what you want to achieve. In fact, this can serve as a useful gauge to measure how much the goal really matters to you. I have a short story that illustrates this point quite well.

Have you ever uttered the words 'I'm never drinking again' after a big night out? I bet you have! I once went on a big road trip to Adelaide with friends to watch my beloved football team play a game. Unfortunately, they lost, but the night was deemed a tremendous success on account of the fun we had. We drove back from Adelaide on Sunday, and I rolled into bed a shadow of myself, got up the next day still feeling rough but functioning fine and headed to work.

When I got home on Monday night, I was so tired that I crashed on the couch in the hope that I could drift off to sleep, but my then one-year-old daughter had other ideas! Eliza came waddling up to me and asked: 'Daddy come play?' to which I replied: 'Sorry darling, Daddy is tired today'.

Then, with pure innocence, my daughter said one thing that literally changed the course of my life: 'That's OK Daddy, I go bed.'

Those six words ripped my heart out of my chest. I had never felt so guilty in my life! I had just dismissed my gorgeous little girl because I was still hungover from Saturday night and, because she was so innocent, she had just accepted my uselessness and waddled away.

Part of my vision for success in my life is being as good a parent as I can possibly be, so when I said that night, 'I'm never drinking again', you'd better believe I had the right reasons to see that through! I had never felt such conviction in a decision, and the energy behind it was a force to be reckoned with (and something that I hadn't felt to that extent before).

In the nine years since that day, not one drop of alcohol has passed these lips. I simply have the right reasons to take me past any temptation in situations in which having a beer would be appropriate or 'nice'. Basically, I would rather be a good dad seven days a week as opposed to only four or five days! That's not to say I won't drink ever again – I like booze – but for now the cost is just not worth it for me. I chose my kids over a few beers, which seems to be pretty obviously the right choice when you look at it like that, right?

If you're looking for more discipline, I recommend that you stop looking for it directly and start looking for the right reasons first, because the discipline will come as a result of having the right reasons and the right vision for success fixed firmly in your head.

What might this success formula look like?

We know that we need the right reasons or motivation to find the required discipline. We also need to accept that failure is part of the process, and that true success is defined by the journey itself, not just by the end result.

If you're still struggling to define success for yourself, maybe try to adapt this to suit your own circumstances: success is felt when the desired outcomes align with your true passions. You can't fake passion, otherwise the discipline won't be there. You can't get that passionate about an outcome that you feel you 'should' aim for as opposed to something you really want to achieve. If you truly want something, then a failure is not likely to knock you off course, either.

Most importantly, you can't be told if something equals success for you; you need to feel it.

Now that we've pondered the meaning of success, let's look at some key topics around it that you will have heard of but may not have understood enough to make them stick in your life.

Chapter 2

Is setting goals the path to your success?

Start with the end in mind.

Stephen R. Covey, *The 7 Habits of Highly Effective People*

(FYI: If you haven't read or listened to this book yet, DO IT!)

You have likely heard about goal setting in various forms and to varying degrees of practicality, and I have no doubt that a bunch of you will have given it a go with varying levels of success.

It's OK if you haven't explored this topic just yet – a lot of people don't realise that they are even allowed to have personal goals! There are lots of books available that can point you in the right direction, but two that I'd recommend you read or listen to (or at least download via Blinkist to get the CliffNotes version!) are *Ready Aim Fire!* by Erik Fisher and Jim Woods, and *Goals!* by Brian Tracy.

If you've tried to set goals for yourself and they haven't quite had the desired effect, then you may have rolled your eyes when seeing this part of the book in the contents page. So many people try to set goals because they were told to, as opposed to setting them because they want to, having understood why they are important and how they can help.

Why is goal setting so important?

Back in 2011, I was really struggling for direction. I had been a salesperson in real estate for eight months. In my first month, I sold three properties, but I had barely done anything after that, with the few sales I came close to making falling through for various reasons.

You could argue that it was due to the threat of a second global financial crisis, which was causing big drops in house prices, but to be honest, the problems were all in my head. I was trying hard enough, but fear of rejection and anxiety around 'pestering people' had me in a bind, and a lack of true understanding had me pinned in a metaphorical corner.

I couldn't see past each day, such was the level of anguish I had around the whole idea of being a salesperson, and I couldn't get over the sales that had fallen through. I took them so personally and my perspective was so warped that failing in my job was defining me as a person.

Then, on a Tuesday morning in July 2011, I had a chance meeting that opened my eyes. Until then I had vaguely heard about goals, but realistically I had no idea how they worked, how to formulate them and why they were so important. A tall, confident American guy by the name of Niik Stewart cruised into our sales meeting. He was on his way to another real estate firm in town, but our CEO had asked him to swing by our office for a chat.

It turns out that Niik has over 130,000 followers on social media and is one of the world's leading sales mindset coaches, so it's safe to say that he knows a thing or two! He told us that he was once on the practice squad for the LA Lakers, and after that he spent a year floundering in sales before working it all out and becoming a tremendous success. Normally my sceptical British mind would be vomiting at the prospect of listening to a guy like Niik, but at that point I was desperate for any sort of answer to the challenges I was facing.

He started by asking: 'Who has goals?'

The next question was: 'Who has their goals written down and in their possession right now?'

A few people in the office had goals, but none of us had anything written down, which caused Niik some concern.

'If you don't write your goals down, then they are nothing but hopes and wishes', he said.

I was shitting myself. Sure, I had stuff coming up that needed to be paid for – a wedding, a house, holidays – but I had not put one ounce of thought into any defined goals, let alone bloody written anything down! Niik said that we wouldn't achieve much at all unless we had something to shoot for, and in my case, he was spot on.

There is a fabled Harvard University study from 1953 that followed a graduating class for ten years. It was discovered that the 3% of students who had written down clear goals had earned ten times more money since graduation than the remaining 97% combined. Unfortunately, there is a bit of conjecture as to the validity of this study (basically, some sales coach back in the day may have made it up to put a few bums onto the seats of their seminar!), but there's another study that actually happened that does demonstrate the significant role goals can play in achieving success.

In 2007, Professor Gail Matthews from Dominican University conducted a study with working professionals from around the world. The participants were divided into five groups with varying levels of goal-setting involvement: some simply thought about their goals, others wrote them down, some created written goals with actionable steps, another group added accountability to a friend, and the final group included all of these elements along with regular progress updates.

The study showed that those who had simply thought about goals achieved around 44% less than their counterparts who had written goals and were accountable to someone other than themselves. Even those people who had just written goals down for themselves performed 33% better than the initial goalless group.

I bought a CD from Niik called 'The 3% Club' and immediately put it on in my car thinking I'd try anything to get myself out of this hole. I followed the guide on goal setting step by step, and I came up with right goals that I was keen on achieving for the remainder of the year and into 2012–13. I had them written down on a small bit of paper and put them in my wallet so that I could read them six to twelve times a day as per the instructions.

The results were profound and immediate. The very next month, I sold six properties, which was six more than I had sold for the entire year to that point. From there, my career in sales kicked on quite well.

I've personally experienced how goals can significantly contribute to your vision of success, turning ambitions into tangible results. This was not only rewarding but also provided valuable lessons that have continued to support my long-term growth as a person.

Niik's impactful lessons led to four immediate improvements to issues I'd been having. If any of the following resonate with you, you'll gain a clearer understanding of the importance of setting goals.

Defeats, let-downs and upsets aren't as upsetting

Goals provide perspective. I used to hold onto every deal so tightly that my knuckles went white because that was all I had to focus on, so if one fell through, I'd be devastated. Once I had goals in place, I had something on the horizon that I could lift my head up and see ahead of me, making that one moment or deal feel a lot less significant in the grand scheme of things.

Have you ever felt like you've built a single event into this edge-of-a-cliff scenario where you almost feel like life is on hold until this event reaches an outcome? I've done that on a number of occasions, to the point where my anxiety rose at the prospect of the wrong outcome coming to pass. But you know what? Irrespective of whether I got the right or wrong result, the sun rose just the same the next day, meaning that this single event was not the be-all and end-all. That's what goals can help you to see.

Reverse-engineering from a detailed vision works

The more detail you assign to your goals, the more useful they become.

In the past, I focused on vague, standard goals like buying a house or car – things that didn't really have a deeper meaning or paint a clear picture for the future. These goals weren't particularly motivating, mostly because they lacked purpose and a timeline. They were more like generic answers I'd give when someone asked about my future plans, rather than goals that genuinely mattered to me.

Without a clear purpose or urgency, it's hard to push beyond the ordinary in your efforts. When there's no timeframe, there's no reason to act today instead of tomorrow. But here's the real issue: how can we achieve anything if we can't even define what we want? You can't define success for yourself if you can't envision living that definition out. As I mentioned earlier, life becomes much more exciting once you take the time to clearly define what success looks and feels like for you.

In *The 7 Habits of Highly Effective People*, Stephen R. Covey refers to this as the 'Start with the end in mind' habit. It's so much easier to work out the feasibility of whatever it is you want to achieve once you've gone through that exercise. I played such a vivid, detailed clip in my mind as to how I wanted life to be that I could feel the texture on the floors and walls of the new house we wanted to live in – it felt real!

Now, here's the tangible benefit to doing this. Once you've gone into that much detail as to your definition of success, you can then put measurable progress markers in place that allow you to define the path to your new horizon. For example, if you want to build a successful business, you can break down the ingredients required to bring that business to life, assign costs in money and time to each element and build a tangible timeline that will get you to your business goal.

A simpler example could be that your dream car (in vivid detail) is a black Range Rover with cream leather interior, tinted windows and a sports package. You go onto the Range Rover website, select the exact options you want and find out the exact cost of the car so that you have a tangible savings target that you need to achieve. Once you have that, you can decide when you want it by and set a goal that will drive you to go get it!

SMART goals make progress

The old acronym SMART (specific, measurable, achievable, relevant, timely) allows you to track how well you are travelling towards achieving your goals. This then helps you to remain accountable to those goals, which gives you either encouragement when you're getting closer or a kick up the arse when you're not!

Why do SMART goals work? There are a few reasons, but for me, a SMART goal feels less like a dream and more like a possibility.

Studies have shown that SMART goals have an active impact on success outcomes when compared to standard goals. Amish Aghera, MD and team published a study in 2018 in which they assessed the efficacy of learning goals depending on whether people had 'normal' goals or SMART goals. The conclusion was that although those with regular targets had no fewer goals than those with SMART goals, the number of actions taken towards achieving their goals was higher in the SMART goals group (1.44 actions per goal) than those taken in the normal goals group (0.87 actions per goal).

It's not like SMART goals are reserved for the mega-driven or uber-ambitious, because we all have at least something that we want to achieve. Because SMART goals make things feel more 'real', the ability to remain internally motivated throughout the process results in more actions being taken towards making these goals a reality. So, even if you have just one goal, bloody well make it a SMART one!

How do you make your goals 'SMART'? Let's start with an example of the difference between a normal (or hopeful) goal as opposed to a SMART goal. A normal goal would be: 'I want a new car'. The SMART version of that would be: 'I will buy a Range Rover Sport, black with cream leather interior, which costs $180,000, by New Year's Eve next year'.

Here's why this goal is SMART:

· The details of the car are Specific.
· The cost, $180,000, is Measurable and Achievable.
· The goal is Relevant to what I want (I want a car).
· The specific deadline makes it Timely.

If you hope to achieve something, ask yourself the following questions:

- What is it **exactly** that I want to achieve?
- How can I **measure** progress along the way?
- **When** do I want to achieve this by? Is this a **realistic** timeframe with the parameters and restrictions I have in my life? **Can I push myself to make this happen**, even with the restrictions currently in place?

The reason why I have those qualifications in the last point is because our goals are supposed to be attainable and realistic, but we need to be pushing our boundaries and not simply acting within our comfort zone. We're never going to achieve more than we already have if we stay in our comfort zone, right?

Reading your goals regularly provides energy

We all have days when motivation is low, but I have found that reading my goals every time I get out of my car helps to frame my mind in a productive way. This simple habit has given me momentum and significantly increased my efficiency with time.

I swear this stuff needs to be taught in schools. I know if it was taught to me back then, I'd have achieved so much more. Instead of pursuing what I thought I needed to achieve – like an engineering degree that I've done nothing with – I could have focused on what I actually wanted to achieve.

Why aren't your goals working?

I personally believe that as necessary as they are, goals can become toxic if you're not careful. This isn't because you don't need them – I believe we all do; even our kids need one or two goals – but if they are mishandled or misinterpreted, or if they are goals that you 'think' you need as opposed to truly desiring, then one of two things generally tends to happen:

1. They start to weigh heavily on your mind, clouding your judgement and grinding your actions to a halt.
2. You become a bit like Gollum from *The Lord of the Rings* and literally sacrifice everything for your 'precious', losing sight of everything else that's going on!

Once upon a time, early on in my sales career, I set myself a goal of reaching $1 million in commissions in 12 months. I hadn't reached $500k before, but for some reason I wanted $1 million, even though I didn't really know anything about what was required. Within a very short period of time, I fell behind in my pursuit and my anxiety levels began to rise significantly. Not only was there tangible distance between where I was and where I needed to be financially, but also I was finding more and more gaps in my understanding, which compounded that feeling of inadequacy.

The resulting pressure turned what was supposed to be a driving inspiration into an anxiety-inducing burden, which is not ideal! Not only had I set an impossible task, I had lost sight of why the goal was important to me. I had become obsessed with the commissions to the point that I was sacrificing catch-ups with friends, time with loved ones and, on occasions, my better judgement. It wasn't pretty, and I actually became quite ill.

Sometimes goals take you away from the things that make you happy. Failing to balance that need to sacrifice with maintaining who you are and what you need can cause greater issues if you're not careful. There's no point reaching your goals if you're in no shape to enjoy the fruits of your labour!

Sometimes our patience runs thin when striving for these goals of ours, so when a chance to speed up the process or make a big jump in progress (or any progress, sometimes) comes along, it's bloody hard to resist the temptation to skip a couple of steps! The problem is that shortcuts very rarely lead to long-term success.

In 2017, I started my freelance auctioneering business as a side project alongside my position as a real-estate sales manager. I loved calling auctions, that's all I wanted to do, so I set an auction volume goal that I wanted to reach by the end of the year. The challenge, though, was that I had only just started the business, so I didn't have many clients to call auctions for! I was so obsessed with reaching my goal number of auctions that I was taking on anyone, anywhere in Melbourne.

Sounds great in theory, but reality soon bit. My 'need' to achieve my goal slowly started to compromise my decision-making as to what constituted 'good business'. Not only was I taking on auctions that were ridiculous distances apart from each other, which lowered the number I could call due to travel times, but a couple of the agents I took on in the early days had… 'interesting' values.

My business nearly unravelled not long after it had been born! I stretched myself way too thin, cost myself other business due to wasting auction time with travel time and, more importantly, compromised my standards by making early connections with characters in the space that everyone would do well to avoid. I risked damaging my reputation, which was still in its infancy at the time, potentially derailing any aspirations I had of becoming the best auctioneer in the industry!

What's the biggest mistake when setting goals?

As I mentioned, goals are great for keeping us accountable, and to make progress we need to push ourselves out of our comfort zones. That's all perfectly healthy. However, many of the top performers in their field often talk about the need to become 'obsessed' with our goals in order to achieve them.

What else do you see as a commonality with these people? More often than not, they drop the ball with their family, make questionable decisions around substances in a bid to get ahead or leave a trail of destruction behind them in their pursuit of their goals.

The trap is that we set goals based on 'ideal world' ideology, which doesn't take into account things like family, kids or any responsibility outside of oneself. A lot of the time, we do that because our social media feeds make us think that 'success' is a walk in the park, so we set goals that excite us, then begin to resent those responsibilities for getting in the way.

If we're being honest with ourselves for a second, a lot of us have gotten frustrated with where we are in our lives, especially when we see something that we want to achieve and then realise that because of the way our life is already set up – marriage, mortgage, kids and so on – what we want is practically unattainable.

Are we allowed to look out for ourselves and what we want? Of course we are! However, we often struggle to balance our desires with the things and people we love. We tend to romanticise what could be and let our fantasies put those we care about at risk of our resentment, which is bullshit!

The lesson here is simple: make sure that your goals are aligned with your life, as well as the way that you (**not** the world) are feeling.

You absolutely need to feel fulfilled with your goals, but setting goals that are impossible in the context of your life situation is going to cause damage to yourself and others. That's not to say that they can't ever happen, but be real with yourself and your time and capacity constraints, and assess whether you may need a bit more time and space in order to make them come to fruition.

Goals should inspire and excite you, making you feel a healthy amount of nervousness about the task ahead. However, they also need to be weighed against any potential impact on your home life. It's crucial to communicate any possible effects to those who may be affected. If you have a partner or someone in your life with a more conservative mindset, their support is essential. Without their buy-in, achieving your goals while maintaining your current set-up will be challenging.

Later in Part I, I'm going to talk about the importance of incremental gains, because it makes achieving your goals feel so much easier and can help you to take your other responsibilities into account. Appreciating the small gains and little wins along the way is a vital part of the process, and reflecting on how far you've travelled towards your goals (as well as on the lessons learned) provides that sense of relief that you've stopped to take it all in before you crack on with the journey.

Chapter 3

How can you stay motivated?

Success is no accident. It is hard work, perseverance, learning, studying, sacrifice and most of all, love of what you are doing or learning to do.

Pelé

WARNING: This chapter is going to talk about a couple of things that you may find confronting. It may give you a nudge and potentially make you face a couple of things that you know you've been avoiding!

For the majority of people, motivation is found via some sort of external stimulus. It's what causes excitement, fear, anticipation, the often-talked-about fight-or-flight response – pretty much any emotion that evokes some sort of action in you. I rely on it during my auction calls! A large part of my craft is to provide an external stimulus that invokes money-spending actions out of buyers in a crowd. It sounds quite manipulative, but all I'm doing is amplifying whatever a buyer is already feeling with words, body language, tonality and, believe it or not, a big smile or three!

The problem is that we can't rely on external stimuli on a day-to-day basis if we want to head towards any level of purposeful success that means something to us.

In 2015–16 I was going OK with work, my family life was good, kiddo number one was healthy and I had a lot of love around me. However, inside I was a mess: I was at a particularly low point in my battle with mental illness, brought about by a lack of identity and a completely self-inflicted fear that I had no real control over my life.

I was looking everywhere for some form of external inspiration to keep me going. I went from watching excitable entrepreneurs like Gary Vaynerchuk to God-fearing Christian preachers. I took any sort of online personality test I could to validate my existence and clambered about the internet trying to find some sort of job that would somehow automatically give me a purpose for my life. I applied for jobs just to feel that I was doing something out of motivation. I even signed up to do a master's degree in a field unrelated to my work, for which I took out a loan, did one semester and dropped out.

I was in a serious hole! And it's not like I was just being a lazy prick. In fact, I was almost the opposite of that because I was firing energy at almost anything I could. No matter what I tried, I could not get out of my own head to build any amount of momentum. What was I searching for? I was chasing any endorphin-inducing activity that validated my existence, that made me feel like I was progressing in some way, shape or form. Have you ever felt that before – when you can't be arsed to go to work, exercise or pretty much do anything? We all cop it at some point or another, and it means we're missing that inner fire that prompts us to get up and crack on.

We could examine any area of our lives to understand this sense of desperation, but let's focus on work for a moment.

Work occupies a significant portion of our lives, and whether we like it or not, a large part of our identity is often tied to our job.

Work to live, live to work – which works?

This seems to be a constant conversation around the dinner table: should we flog our guts out in order to pay bills, take a holiday, buy a car and have the stuff, or should we just earn 'enough' while pursuing something more fulfilling, spending time with the kids and 'having a life'?

I have a huge problem with this whole concept, and so should you! Why? Because work doesn't happen separately to life; it is a part of your life whether you like it or not! This whole work-life balance question contributes to the negativity, because it pits one against the other when they should be complementing each other.

If you look at the argument more closely, it's not as clearly defined as the standard rhetoric suggests, anyway. Although we are ultimately defined by the choices we make, sometimes the collective outcome of a series of decisions puts us into situations that we really don't like.

See if you recognise yourself in any of the following situations. It always helps if you understand where you currently stand so you can identify where you want to be.

No work, no life

This category of people has little income and no real spark in life to get excited about. Some are OK to simply exist, live pay cheque to pay cheque and function through each day, which is entirely their prerogative. However, if you're reading this book and you find yourself in this position, then you'll likely be desperate to get out of the hole you feel that you're in, which is totally understandable.

Before you start, don't go blaming yourself or anyone around you for being in this position! Part of your drama is likely to come from resentment, regret or anger based on past circumstances, events or decisions, which is a complete fucking waste of time. For once, just put the anchor of blame down, get your shit together and give yourself permission to look forward to what could be instead of what has already been.

Life over work

People who value life over work and are perceived to 'work to live'. They value life over monetary gain and see fulfilment outside of the material.

What a lot of people miss is that people in this category are then split between those with purpose and those without. Those without purpose really aren't fussed about earning money or committing to a career – they just want a job to pay for stuff they want and things they do, and they're happy to operate within their financial limitations. If you have purpose in this category, though, you're committed to a path irrespective of the cost, which is great for you but can also be costly to loved ones or those around you. I've been one of these people! I could have been earning a lot more money, but I'd have been way less entertained. It was great for me but caused anxiety for those around me.

Work over life – the workaholic

I've been a workaholic too! This group gets a bad reputation because they work at the expense of their own wellbeing for the benefit of others. Golden handcuffs can also keep these individuals chained to their job, with their lifestyle or financial commitments preventing them from pursuing a change that better aligns with their life.

Sometimes, it's an obsession with the work itself or an overly committed attitude that can negatively impact other areas of life. This can become quite isolating if you're not careful. I've experienced this firsthand – working intensely without a connection to a greater purpose can lead to a lot of resentment.

When purpose, work and life align

For this group of people, everything is in proportion. This is when you don't need to have a work-life balance because you love what you do and you live the life that makes you happy. This doesn't necessarily mean that you're loaded with cash, but you've got work to a position that allows you and your loved ones to have a great time in life.

There is a degree of luck involved in this. For example, the skill that you're incredibly passionate about and happen to be great at could either be something like driving Formula 1 cars, which makes you millions and takes you around the world, or it could be balancing a spoon on the end of your nose, which is a cool party trick but ain't going to pay the bills!

However, even if your particular talent is a useless party trick, if your purpose, work and life all flow in harmony then you can consider yourself to be winning in this game of life.

If you want to make any change in your life, though, you're going to need to put in the work. When you're uninspired by your current circumstances then you're not going to be able to rely on ra-ra motivational speeches and quotes that you find online! You're going to need to find that spark, so let's have a look at the elements that go into creating motivation from within ourselves to get shit done.

Internal vs external motivation

It's easy to be motivated in the short term by 'stuff'. For instance, look at how game shows use a new car or money to motivate the audience. However, it's often much harder to stay motivated when there are no 'external' stimulants to nudge us along. It's why YouTube has billions of views on all these motivational videos that tell you to 'go get it' and 'stop being a little bitch' with some guy running 1000 km or pushing crazy amounts of weight in a gym, because we can't seem to find that motivation ourselves.

What do we need to do to light that internal spark? Self-determination theory (SDT) refers to a person's own ability to manage themselves, to make confident choices and to think on their own. It encompasses things like key personality traits and motivation, and within that, determines that there are three basic requirements to feel internally or 'intrinsically' motivated:

1. **Autonomy** – we want to be in control of what we're doing and what's happening around us.
2. **Competence** – we need to feel that we can tackle challenges, both in terms of the tasks we're handling and the people involved.
3. **Relatedness** – we need to feel connected to the task and/or other people in a meaningful way.

When we feel confident in our skills, comfortable with the people we're working with and able to move at our own pace, we're on the right track. Adding the excitement of being challenged by a meaningful goal can ignite that inner drive, making you less reliant on external motivation like YouTube clips.

So, now that we've assessed where we currently stand and identified the elements needed to fuel our inner fire, you might be looking for this book to provide a way out of feeling trapped.

If your social media feed is flooded with people talking about 'chasing your passion' and highlight reels of people effectively 'living the dream', it may make you feel even more strongly like you can't escape from your current situation. This is such a common frustration that so many people experience, and I can talk to it with a good degree of accuracy because I've got the t-shirt for it!

The thing with passion is that it's bandied around so much we almost don't feel like it's a real concept anymore, but the power that passion can give you to blast out of dark places cannot be replicated. Taking steps to find your passion may make you feel awkward and uncomfortable at first, but those feelings are a sign that you're exploring something new, so they're a good sign of progress.

There are many ways to discover your passion, but one straightforward approach is outlined in an article on the platform Calm. It presents five simple steps to help you find, pursue and sustain your passion:

1. **Self-reflect.** Think about your hobbies, what you're naturally good at and what puts a smile on your face.

2. **Do your homework.** If you're interested in trying something new, start by researching what it would take to make it happen – consider the steps involved, the time commitment and the financial costs. Be realistic – this passion won't just come to you effortlessly, and it might take years to become a central part of your life.

3. **Test and learn.** What have we said about failure? It helps us to progress towards success, and success in finding your passion is likely to come only after finding a few dead ends first.

4. **Connect to those who are already 'in the game'.** There's nothing better than talking to people who are already in the

world that you want to get into, so reach out, show some admiration and ask for permission to question them about their journey. You'll learn a lot from them that you won't find online.

5. **Be consistent and committed to the search.** This isn't going to happen overnight, so give yourself permission to spend a bit of time every day digging for that golden passion and the process or path you're going to need to take.

I implore you to start feeling around for a passion right now before you become disillusioned. If you find one, allow yourself a moment to dream about how it would feel to make a living from that passion in some way, directly or otherwise. Next, set some goals around it and work towards them incrementally. If you can't find a passion that has any vague opportunity to become a source of motivation for you, don't panic, and don't force yourself to be passionate about something. Your gut will call you out on your lies rather quickly!

If you still think that I'm preaching from an ivory tower, then I need to remind you of this truth: if you want to make a change, you can't use your current reality as an excuse.

If you're determined to make a change but you're juggling an eight-hour workday, kids, bills and other responsibilities, instead of complaining about your situation, accept your reality and find a way to work around it. Do you really think anyone magically fell into their dream role that aligned with their passions and personality? Any significant shift requires a substantial amount of energy, but when you find a passion that can potentially become a way of living, that energy isn't difficult to muster.

When I took the chance of opening an auction business, I had a mortgage, one child and another on the way, two car loans, a 10- to 12-hour workday (six days a week) and all the bills that came with living in as expensive a city as Melbourne. Could I change that? Nope! But because I had found my true passion, I looked at how I could work around my situation, which resulted in me waiting until kiddo was in bed and getting to work until the early hours of the following morning for a year while I continued with my current role. After that, I had finally built it to a point that allowed me to jump 'full-time' into my passion in 2018.

What does that mean for you? If you truly want it enough, you will have to find a way of carving out the time and energy to make it happen, because no one is going to just hand it to you on a silver platter. You are responsible for digging yourself out of the hole you find yourself in. The amazing thing is that if you have found your passion, you'll find a way somehow; the energy will be there within you, waiting to come roaring out!

What is the power of consistency?

Success isn't just about greatness; it's about consistency. As Dwayne 'The Rock' Johnson said, 'Consistent hard work leads to success. Greatness will come'. Strength isn't built from occasional effort, and you can't learn skills like driving or fitness without regular practice. Just as soccer teams and ballet dancers don't perform without rigorous preparation, achieving excellence in any field requires unwavering dedication.

When you discover your passion, you become deeply invested and naturally motivated, tapping into new levels of discipline and energy. For me, mastering auctioneering meant practising daily, studying scripts, expanding my vocabulary and learning about body language. If your current life set-up feels like a barrier to pursuing your passion, remember: every great achievement starts with consistent, focused effort, even if the path ahead looks daunting.

The last time I checked, climbing Mount Everest is a rigorous process that requires extensive preparation and training. Prospective climbers undergo years of training to qualify for the expedition. Specifically, it's recommended to dedicate 8 to 11 weeks of training solely to reaching Base Camp.

The physical challenge of climbing the biggest mountain in the world is somewhat obvious, and therefore the route to the summit can be envisioned with relative ease. However, when it comes to summits, passions or goals, the scale of the task in front of us to reach where we want to be can in fact be a lot more overwhelming than scaling the tallest peak in the world. That's not an exaggeration, either – as you read this you could well be experiencing a build-up of anxiety at the prospect of attempting to achieve a goal or engage in a passion for yourself.

Do you think that I instantly became the number-one auctioneer in Australia by simply picking up a gavel and shouting? If I entered into a competition or threw my name into the hat, I'd have been laughed out of the room! It took thousands of hours of practice and over a thousand auctions to even get close, but of course I couldn't have done all of that with one big effort – it took gradual improvement over time.

The whole concept of incremental gains was brought to light by the legendary Sir Dave Brailsford, who took over an awful cycling team that hadn't won a thing and turned them into perennial Tour de France champions. Instead of trying to leap to the top of a mountain in one go, Sir Dave figured that it'd be much easier to break down the task into its individual components and focus on improving each element by 1%. He broke down the scale of the improvement into the most tangible little progressions, even to the point that he had the pillows that riders slept on tested for their comfort and support!

Improving individual things by just 1% sounds much easier than trying to win a Tour de France in one go, but such was the rate of overall improvement by adding all of the 1% gains together that the team became a success almost overnight.

So, instead of looking at your goals as huge, insurmountable tasks, why don't you set the path to victory and then just focus on getting 1% closer each day? Or 1% stronger? The maths of this shows that if you were to get 1% stronger every day for a year, then you would end up with an aggregate improvement of 37 times your original level!

To improve by 1% each day is not even remotely scary, and it's way more reasonable for you to achieve, even with the pressures of the real world on your shoulders. There will be days when you have a chance and the drive to improve by more than 1%, and other days when 1% sounds like the most painful thing ever. However, even with the responsibilities that come with daily life, it's always possible to carve out a small amount of time to make progress toward your mountain peak.

Remember to set goals, work out the path to victory, then focus on getting a little bit closer each day. It may take a little longer, but you'll get there.

When is enough... enough?

I have a problem with the need to feel satisfaction. In fact, I have a few problems with it, and it ties in with why we need to see success in the progress within the process, as opposed to setting it against a finite outcome.

Do you ever feel like you're constantly searching for satisfaction in life? You set a goal, you achieve it, but then you're left wondering, 'Is this really it?'

I spent so many years getting frustrated because every time I accomplished something, I had conditioned myself to always be looking ahead for the next thing instead of feeling a sense of success. Satisfaction is always seen in the future, and for so long I beat myself up for not being able to catch up to it.

In auctioneering terms, it didn't matter how well I did, I was never satisfied – I would always dwell on what could have been done better. This can be seen as a positive when chasing greater levels of success, but it can't be sustained forever, and you are likely to end up fried like I was.

My intense (and it was intense) confusion around the whole topic of satisfaction reached a peak in the early part of 2020. As well as my auctioneering business, I had started a marketing business and a charity support service to try and provide some sort of satisfaction in my working life. And then it all changed, but not for the reason the rest of the world had at the time.

While I was sitting with my dad in the hospital in his final days, despite all the activity, the beeps from the machinery and various TVs playing faintly in the background, all I could hear was the strained effort of his breathing. Unfortunately, as a result of a stroke, along with mobility problems, my dad also lost the ability to speak, which meant that neither Mum, my brother Rob nor I got to have a final conversation with the man who was supposed to always be the pillar of strength for our family.

As I sat there listening to his breathing, there was one question that I wish I had a chance to ask him: 'Dad, are you satisfied with how your life played out?'

It was a question that I pondered at length. My old man had been dealt a rough hand in life but somehow managed to create a life of service, initially in the army and then the police force. He raised two boys that have both ended up OK in their own right, and he had become the best granddad to four grandkids. He was loved and respected by everyone, and even my mates called him 'Big Jim' on account of his popularity.

But it was in those final days that Dad taught me something that lifted a weight off my shoulders and brought a whole new perspective to how life needs to be perceived when it comes to satisfaction.

What I realised was that while there is still time left in the game of life, there are always going to be chances to improve (or lose) the amount of satisfaction that we have in our lives. Simply put, until that final curtain is drawn, there will always be time to nail that last monologue or cock up that last line! Or, in my dad's case, until you're about to tap out, you can't really answer whether you're satisfied with life or not.

British philosopher Alan Watts makes a profoundly simple observation about chasing satisfaction. He uses the English language to point out that it is futile to chase whatever is 'there' because by the time you get 'there' it becomes 'here', so you can never make it 'there' and must look at the joy you find 'here' where you currently stand.

I realised that you can chase satisfaction all you want, but it'll never be enough because there will always be something over 'there' for you to chase after. The relief in understanding that satisfaction is a long-term game (or the longest-term game!) gives us permission to withhold any finite judgement as to whether we've succeeded or not. It also provides opportunities to consistently improve on where we find ourselves in a particular skill set, or even in life.

But it does beg the question: if satisfaction is impossible to achieve unless you are at the end of a particular body of time (whether it is death, retirement or after any significant endpoint in your life), how can we feel any joy in the progress that we've made?

Why is it so difficult to be 'present'?

You've probably heard the phrase 'stop and smell the roses'. This advice is meant to encourage being 'present' and in the moment. But, for someone who gets anxious at the thought of sitting still, it can be incredibly irritating. Whenever I'm told to stop and smell the roses, the word 'stop' triggers an allergic reaction. It's part of that conditioning I mentioned earlier – life moves so fast that pausing feels counterproductive.

Being present is tough with constant notifications and alerts disrupting our focus. I once had an Apple Watch, but it only added to my anxiety with its constant interruptions. Sure, you can enable 'Do Not Disturb', but how many of us actually do this consistently? Eckhart Tolle talked about this challenge when he said: 'Most humans are never fully present in the now, because unconsciously they believe that the next moment must be more important than this one. But then you miss your whole life, which is never not now'. If you're familiar with him, you know staying focused on his teachings can be a feat in itself, as he seems to operate on almost zero energy, he is so laid back. However, if you can stick with it, his insights on presence are profoundly impactful.

And that is why we need to take a second to understand where we are in our lives at any given moment. If we don't, we'll miss life as it is now and never get a chance to enjoy everything that we live and work for, which isn't an incentive to achieve much!

It's not just about savouring the good times

Later in the book, we look at how to manage yourself when the shit hits the fan, but when it comes to success, being present not only prevents you from getting ahead of yourself, it can also help you to focus on tasks while you're struggling with other parts of your life.

Ultimately, you can only do what you can right now to enact real change. Another popular phrase for this is, 'You can only control what you can control'. So, if you find yourself with your back against the wall, being present is more often than not the only option you have left.

Whenever I analyse any of my auction calls, although I'm never satisfied, I'm a lot more balanced in my review. I do recognise some stuff that I do quite well now, as well as picking out the various little things that I could tweak should a similar situation arise.

The beautiful thing about my craft is there is no such thing as the perfect auction call. We're dealing with the subjectivity of human beings who are all wired differently, all 8.1 billion of them! There will always be things to learn, cultural nuances to understand and dynamics to read within the context of my line of work.

While 'contentment' is often seen as a synonym for satisfaction, for me, being content with your work means being pleased with your progress while recognising that there's always more to achieve. Unlike satisfaction, which feels final, contentment keeps the door open for ongoing improvement and future learning.

In the context of success and recognising that the journey is where success truly lies, it makes sense that we shouldn't cling to the need for satisfaction, as Mick Jagger might. Instead, we should let go of that need and focus on the ongoing flow of contentment throughout our process towards achieving our goals.

A life lesson in being present

When I was in college, we had a notoriously grumpy rugby coach by the name of Tony Rolt. Mr Rolt was extremely direct, didn't hold anything back and you always knew where you stood with him. His candour made him one of the most popular and most respected teachers in school. I remember it was his off-the-field advice that gave me much-needed mental and emotional relief when I was at a particularly low point.

I was in my final year in 2001, and my dad discovered that he might have prostate cancer. This hit me hard and threw me into a world of doubt. Your dad's supposed to be invincible and, all of a sudden, you realise he is mortal.

Mr Rolt had taken over as my housemaster and, as I was boarding in my final year, we spent some time in each other's company away from rugby. When he heard about my dad, he took me into his office and asked how I was doing. Then he gave me the following advice that has served me well to this day:

Reidy, there's nothing I can say that is going to change how you feel or what's happening with your dad. Whether you like it or not, there's nothing you can do about it either. What I can offer you is a space to focus on something else. If you don't feel like playing against Worksop on Saturday, that's understandable, but playing rugby will give you a chance to put your worries down and just be you for 80 minutes.

Once you cross that white line, nothing else matters. While you're on that pitch, you can't do anything for your dad or your mum, and all you have are your teammates and the game. No doubt your worries will be waiting for you when the game's over, but you will at least have had some relief from them.'

Talk about profound. I had so much going on at the time with the end of college coursework and exams, representing the school at rugby, acting in a play and I was also a senior prefect, with other responsibilities around the school. I was at that age when understanding girls was like solving the Da Vinci Code; in fact getting a girlfriend was pretty much Mission Impossible!

But here's the point; even though my dad was fronting up in a serious health battle, everything else in my life was going to happen regardless. Mr Rolt explained to me that while I was playing rugby, all I had to do was focus on rugby, because there was no chance that I could be doing anything else in that moment.

This lesson has continued to carry me through various challenges in my life, allowing me to compartmentalise problems and focus purely on what is in front of me, giving me the headspace to continue with my other commitments and keep my world turning.

It's not as if I didn't care for dad, but allowing the rest of my world to crumble wasn't going to help him – it could well have made his illness worse. Sometimes concentrating on the present, even when other things are in turmoil, means we can keep functioning when the rest of the world is still turning.

Chapter 4

What else impacts success?

I love money. I love everything about it.
I bought some pretty good stuff. Got me a $300 pair
of socks. Got a fur sink. An electric dog polisher.
A gasoline powered turtleneck sweater. And, of course,
I bought some dumb stuff, too.

Steve Martin, comedian

I've talked a bit about what success is and how to achieve it, but there are some other factors to take into account on your journey to success. This chapter explores how various factors – money, time, loyalty and technology – can affect your success journey.

Rewriting your relationship with money

Lots of people are 'all about the money', others pick life over money, and some focus on value. Until recently, I had dismissed the importance of money and had a negative relationship with it because I felt hamstrung by expectations I had burdened myself with.

In late 2017, I had a choice that had a tremendous effect on the money I was earning. I had been running my auction business part-time (five to six hours a day) for ten months and it had grown to a point where it needed more than part-time hours. I wasn't earning a huge amount of money from it, but it made me feel alive!

At the time, I was thriving as a salesperson and manager. Almost every home I went into I listed, properties were selling well, and the team was beginning to do good numbers now that teammates like my good friend Jo were really firing as well. I also had a share of the business and had been working with my father-in-law for seven years, so job security was assured. I was working regular 16- to 17-hour days, my daughter Eliza was three and needed attention, and my then-wife was being neglected... something had to give!

I felt that it was clearly a decision of passion versus money, which is a crossroads that most of us meet at some point if we want to make our passion our mainstay in life. If I had my time over, I may have worked out how I could maintain both, but at that moment it needed to be one or the other.

My problem with money was that I felt trapped by the expenses I had accumulated – mortgage, cars, holidays – all of which I had grown accustomed to. I had effectively locked myself into golden handcuffs, which kept me confined to my role. When I discovered my passion and saw my skills and reputation as an auctioneer growing, the decision was clear: I needed to escape what felt like a self-imposed financial prison.

While I absolutely love the decision I made, and looking back I am so glad about the journey it took me on, I think that I made a critical mistake in my theory about money, and sharing it may help you in your decision-making process.

My parents were both police officers from a young age and worked really hard to earn a living. They served the community in one of the most important ways possible and took home a standard pay cheque that didn't reflect the literal blood, sweat and tears they poured into their roles. They were an integral part of the system, but as a result always had a limited amount of money each month to live on. When it came to me, they sacrificed so much to make sure that I wanted for nothing and took out another mortgage on the family home in order to put me through a good school. They were incredible parents, and I'm so immensely thankful for the upbringing that they provided for me.

The challenge in my family was a constant concern over how much money we had. I remember Big Jim (a.k.a. Dad) frequently complaining about our financial situation, leading to many heated debates about money. Other than opportunities for overtime, there weren't many ways to increase our income, making the sacrifices they made for me even more significant. While we weren't living in poverty – we had holidays, were well-fed and dressed well – money was often the focal point of arguments.

What I've discovered since looking into this for myself is that my parents (or, more specifically, my dad) had been brought up with a scarcity mindset around money, which is totally understandable given their upbringing and workplace structure. This had naturally transposed my train of thought and, as a result, it wouldn't matter how much money I earned, it would never be enough. This caused me to harbour a distinct dissatisfaction with money. It made me feel bad however much I earned, and despite the amount of cool stuff it had afforded me and my family, I quite frankly resented it!

Breaking that mindset wasn't easy, but it taught me to discern which opportunities are truly worth investing in.

My auctioneering career has taken me across the country, and I'm always willing to invest in experiences that enhance my craft. For me, the question isn't whether I can afford something; it's how I can make it happen.

From my observations of society (and myself), there appear to be a few different energies or mindsets around money, and they appear to be quite cyclical:

- **Freedom from concern** – brought about by a complete disconnect with material goods
- **Necessity** – the need to satisfy the necessities in life
- **Scarcity** – you never have enough
- **Contentment** – you're happy with your lot
- **Resentment** – disdain towards those with money (brought about via jealousy)
- **Striving** – making efforts to achieve more
- **Abundance** – money is always available to own or obtain
- **Freedom from concern** – brought about by a disconnect with money because they already have more than enough!

The main thing we all need to get comfortable with is this: money is not the enemy. Our interpretation of what it represents determines the role it plays in our lives. Whether we like it or not, money does actually make the world go round, and it provides opportunities that other things simply cannot. It is our energy towards it that is reflected back at us.

I see these energies play out during auctions all the time, and not just with bidders as you may expect, because agents often show me their relationship with money through the actions they take during an auction. Identifying which mindset the customers are in (whether it's owners or buyers) is quite important when working out how best to assist and encourage. For example, the nervous bidders generally hold a scarcity mindset, because they feel that they're up against it from the start, and that can translate as a weakness to their fellow bidders. Conversely, a bidder who exudes confidence can often make others feel inadequate before they reach their financial limit for a particular property. This understanding of mindset and energy reflects a broader principle of success: it's not just about financial resources but about leveraging psychological insights and proactive strategies to achieve your goals.

As you navigate your own journey, consider this gut-check: if your initial reaction is 'Can I...?' it may indicate that the opportunity doesn't align with your goals. But if your first thought is 'How do I...?' it suggests a determination to find a way forward. This shift in perspective can help you stay focused on evolving and achieving your own goals.

Understanding the value of your time

I've lost count of the number of times I've uttered the words 'I've not got time', and I'm sure you have too. Time is the only commodity we can't replicate or replace, and yet I'm quite confident that despite how precious it is, we are all guilty of wasting so much of it.

Whether at work or at home, one of the biggest detractors to our performance is the challenge we face on a daily basis around efficiency. Whether it's due to operational issues, laziness, lack of energy or simply overcommitment, every person reading this book will have efficiency issues in one part of their lives, but we spend so much more of our time talking about money because, like climbing a mountain, it's tangible. Is it because we think time is free? Is it because we are automatically spending time from the minute we're born until the second we die?

When aiming to achieve our goals, reach a higher level of performance and become 'successful', it's common to struggle with breaking old habits that have become ingrained in our psyche. So, what can we do – or at least be mindful of – to improve our chances of becoming more efficient?

Time (excuse the pun) for an admission – my business model is rubbish! It's not because I'm not providing a service of value. As the best auctioneer in the country, I like to think (and prove on a regular basis) that my presence in an auction equates to a substantial uptake in fortunes and income for all concerned in the transaction!

The major problem is this: any business that only sells human-to-human services is essentially selling their time, which automatically limits the amount of revenue it can generate. In other words, I can only fit so many auctions into my diary each weekend, so once that capacity is reached, my ability to make any more money drops to zero. Not ideal!

As you slowly formulate and execute your plan to be more successful, you will find that your time becomes increasingly limited. This is where you will find a significant mental hurdle that causes a lot of people to stumble, myself included.

What is your time worth?

When I first started freelance auctioneering in 2017, my rate per auction was $495. I had intentions to increase that by $100 per year to account for increased demand and rising costs until I hit a ceiling. This is what happened instead:

- 2017 = $495
- 2018 = $595
- 2019 = $595 (the market turned and it got harder for agents, so I decided to keep this rate for a year)

- 2020 = $595 (the pandemic hit everyone, so I thought I couldn't possibly raise my fee this year)
- 2021 = $595 (everyone was recovering from the pandemic, including me, but I still couldn't raise my rate)
- 2022 = $595 (sure, petrol prices were rising, as was my mortgage, and my food bill… but still…)
- 2023 = $695 (FINALLY! Only took four fucking years!)

Considering that during that time I had grown to be one of the most active auctioneers in Victoria, repped on the auction committee of the state real-estate institute, won the state auction-eering title in 2020 (as well as an industry contribution award), made top six in the Australasian competition scene and been crowned Australian Auctioneer of the Year, why didn't I raise my fee? I had all the evidence I could possibly need of my worth, and my capacity was maxing out on the weekend, which meant that I only had one way to increase my income and I didn't take it.

Sounds ridiculously stupid, right? Here's where the challenge lies: unless you have the arrogance and financial ability to lose a volume of business and not be concerned, increasing your fee is a massive challenge. As well as this, there's no manual or guide to help you put any sort of valuation on your time, so how are you going to know what's right?

If you're starting a business or have intentions to sell your time in any way, then this question needs a lot more consideration than we might think. Not only that, but you need to put some work into the ownership of that value, because it is going to be challenged! Even if you're an employee, you need to have an understanding of what your time is worth to the company and the value of the contribution you're providing.

When we talk about valuing our time, it's not just monetary. Neuro-performance scientist Dr Kristy Goodwin gave me a scary example of this in our chat on my podcast when she described wanting to commit her time to her kids but getting distracted by emails. She had been away on a work trip and returned home to her young son, who understandably wanted extra 'mummy cuddles'. Her inbox was awash with stuff that she had missed while she was away, and Kristy had made the mistake of opening it while she had her little one around. The distraction from the email avalanche caused Kristy to miss her son taking a fall and kissing the floor with his face, leaving him with a scar that he has to this day. (Full disclosure, the cut was a reopened cut from an accident that kiddo had sustained while being under Dad's supervision. Kristy would kill me if I didn't make note of that!)

Kristy recognised that the value of the time she spends with her kids far outweighs any potential distraction that work could throw her way. You'll also need to make that distinction when you're setting boundaries, as it's essential for keeping the right perspective on what's truly important to you!

What is the cost of wasted time?

This might shock you into action! Whether you're in a salaried role, a commission-based position, unemployed but looking for work or working for yourself, quantifying your time in monetary terms makes the need for better time management way more tangible.

If you were to just look at your time spent in work, you'd be relatively shocked. A productivity study by David Finkel's company Maui Mastermind measured the time spent on non-productive or low-value activities by business leaders when operating within their business and discovered that in a standard working week, leaders spent an incredible 21.8 hours on stuff they either should be handing off or cutting out entirely! If you multiplied those

21.8 hours by the average hourly rate in Australia as of 2024 ($43.06), then we'd be spending $938.71 each week wasting time. Scary, right?

And that's just the time wasted at work. You can imagine how much that figure would increase for time wasted outside of work! Now, this isn't to say that we should never relax and 'waste' time on the couch, for example, but this highlights the need to ensure that as best as you can, you have a degree of purpose with each action you take.

If you need a break or want to chill out on the couch, that's absolutely fine. However, if you work out your own hourly rate, you will very quickly start to question whether you really need to rewatch an entire season of *Downton Abbey* on a Sunday or, more likely, whether you really need to be scrolling through your social media feeds for an hour at a time. I mean, they say that smoking is an expensive addiction, but if you add up all of that scrolling time online, I'm not sure those TikToks are worth the hundreds of dollars you're spending on them with your time!

Define your time by setting boundaries

'Gotta hustle every minute of the day' is a standard rhetoric fired out by alpha males on their Instagram Reels to butch up their work efforts and make them feel like they're getting the shit done that you won't do. The insistence that your life needs to be about work has been so overwhelming that a huge part of society now struggles to differentiate between working hard and enslavement!

I mentioned the need to set boundaries when it comes to the tasks you need to do to make money and gain a degree of success, but we need to understand the importance of setting boundaries in everything that we do, otherwise we'll just be at the mercy of everything and everyone. In business terms, if you fly by the seat of your pants and let your life pull you from one thing to another, or jump at the whim of clients, you won't have a sustainable or scalable business.

Setting boundaries doesn't necessarily mean that you need to become selfish or rude to anyone; it's actually the opposite, because you're setting expectations and therefore creating clarity for those around you, whether that's clients, colleagues, kids or your partner. It means that when you are with them, you really can commit to being present.

The COVID-19 pandemic really caused a problem with this when we all got locked in our own homes. A research article published by *Frontiers in Psychology* studied and cross-studied the negatives of working from home brought about by the 'blurring of lines' between professional and personal life. Not only did it show that not setting boundaries lowered happiness, but it also prevented people from sustaining a healthy lifestyle and created 'emotional exhaustion'. If we want to be successful, we kind of need all of those things!

I'm confident that a lot of you will know exactly what I mean when I mention the word 'guilt' when it comes to committing to a task instead of spending time with the kids or doing something that would be deemed 'useful' to others. When brand strategist Amanda Delosa joined me on the podcast, she talked about her learning experiences when it came to setting boundaries, having recently become a mum. One of the first things that she gave herself permission to do was set up a structure and boundaries that were going to work for her family, not following the standard family format that society (and those around her) assumed she'd adopt.

She set up her business in a separate part of the house so that she could still 'go to work', organised childcare at home so that she could still be around if required, and scheduled her time so that she could reason with the mum-guilt and commit her time to her public relations business. That allowed her to be a mum when it was time to be a mum, because setting boundaries with your time sets boundaries in your mind.

Are you a slave to the game or a servant of the game?

If you don't have control over your time, you can very quickly be at the mercy of it and completely miss your obligations in certain elements of your life. In business, it's understandable that you'd drop whatever you're doing for a meeting with a potential customer. The challenge is that if you remain reactionary to the whim of the customer, you'll not get very much else done because you'll never be able to commit.

The good news is that if you respect and protect your time, your customers will respect it too, and you can apply this to all elements of your life. Not long after my daughter Eliza was born, I realised that I was very much a slave to my sales role in that I was unnecessarily sacrificing a lot of time for potential clients instead of spending time with my baby girl.

When Eliza was six months old, her mum was ready to go back to work for a day or two. Recognising that I hadn't spent a lot of time with Eliza up to that point, my wife issued me with the ultimatum that every other Wednesday I must take a day off to be with Eliza, otherwise she'd be getting looked after by our dog for the day! This forced me to say no to clients who asked to see me on those Wednesdays. Surprisingly, any client that I told I couldn't meet because I was on 'dad duties' was absolutely fine with it! They happily scheduled a time and day that worked for me. It was a huge realisation that I was in control of my time and I didn't have to be a complete slave to my work. The incredible byproduct of making this change was that it showed people I valued my time, which earned a degree of respect from potential clients and actually contributed to a higher conversion rate despite restricting my availability.

If you don't respect your time, how can you expect anyone else to? That applies to your work life as well as your home life. The most successful people in the world respect their time more than anything else.

Is being loyal a waste of time these days?

When the world is moving so fast, many of us worry that staying in one place for too long – whether it's work, a location or relationship – will hold us back from achieving success. Yahoo! Finance reported on a study by CareerBuilder that found the average job tenure has decreased with each generation. For example, Gen Z typically stays in a role for an average of just two years and three months, with 40% of them holding more than one job or role at once.

Now, I can hear the standard narrative from you about this already, depending on your age. If you're north of 40 you're arguing that 'young people' have no staying power and are unable to handle any level of adversity. If you're under 30, you're telling me that you're sick of not being listened to. Am I close? The truth is somewhere in the middle. When you consider the factors that have caused this concept to evolve, it's easy to see why opinions on this value vary so widely.

How does loyalty differ between generations?

Loyalty can be defined in various ways, but it fundamentally involves four key traits: commitment, trust, faith and consistency.

It's not like the value of loyalty has been completely lost by society, and to be honest, I don't think you can blame one particular generation for it. However, the interpretation of it has most certainly evolved as a result of people's shifting areas of focus. For Gen X, although they are stereotypically the most cynical, they love the consistency and therefore predictability of sticking with what they know. Gen Z, on the other hand, have been brought up in a transactional, dispensable society, which is why they like to pin their identity to a greater cause that aligns more with their passions.

In a professional sense, operating with greater social responsibility is of greater importance to Gen Z than any other generation, according to a survey conducted by Australian recruitment firm Xref. If the business operates with a clear conscience, then Gen Z will be more likely to be loyal to it.

What erodes loyalty?

So, what are the contributing factors towards disdain or apathy towards loyalty?

- **Living in a 'throwaway' society:** In Western cultures, the rise of single-use items has diminished the value we place on material goods. My major vice is coffee made with those disposable pods; as an example of this throwaway mentality we've adopted, GreenMatch in the UK reported that a whopping 56 BILLION of these coffee pods end up in landfill every year! This throwaway mentality extends across multiple parts of society, be it divorce rates, job length, car ownership or almost anything significant. Such trends reflect a broader conditioning to remain less attached to things, reflecting a shift in how we view and value our possessions.

- **More access to revenue generation than ever:** The days when securing a job in a traditional business was essential for survival are long gone. Today, generating income is easier than ever, with many people juggling multiple roles to create a diverse income stream. For instance, Uber reported a significant 24.56% increase in its driver pool in 2024, reaching 7.1 million drivers, many of whom use it to supplement their primary income. This increased ability to make money has led younger generations to seek greater purpose in their work because they're less likely to be susceptible to the golden handcuffs of a job. That's really hard for older generations to accept because the message of working hard and persisting with one job or role was drilled into them, and so they have grown this perspective that young people simply don't work as hard (even though they show that they do by holding down multiple roles at once).

· **Greater importance on 'self' rather than the collective:** At this risk of shooting myself in the foot here, WordsRated reported that as of 2020, the self-help book industry was worth US$10.5 billion, with an estimated 15,000 titles published each year, and the market was tipped to rise to US$14 billion by 2025. The insane amount of focus on the notion of 'self' has conditioned many of us to focus on what we can do by ourselves as opposed to what can be achieved by the collective in a team environment. The use of 'self' as a prefix has shot up exponentially since the turn of the century, and almost everywhere you turn there are campaigns that are trying to push society down the path of self-reflection and self-care in the micro, as is shown in the incredible rise of the self-care industry.

The benefits to being loyal to yourself and others

With the current state of the world, what is the point of demonstrating or exuding loyalty?

The ability to be agile and make quick decisions is undoubtedly important, but the ability to be loyal in life has so many benefits too. Self-loyalty represents a commitment to your values, integrity and goals, and your behaviours in one area of your life do end up being reflected in other areas of your life.

If you don't practice loyalty in some way, you might be setting yourself up for a harder path to success. Our habits significantly influence our behaviours and personality traits, so if we compromise our loyalty in one area of our lives, it's likely to affect our loyalty in other areas as well. Essentially, a lack of loyalty in one area can lead to a broader pattern of inconsistency and difficulty in achieving long-term success.

Loyalty also accelerates the return level of commitment from the people you are being loyal to. A study from Newson, Buhrmester and Whitehouse talks about the obvious loyalty when committing to a group identification through thick and thin (more thin than thick when you're a Newcastle United fan!) and associated benefits of sacrifice and safety in numbers. It also talks about 'identity fusion', which is the notion that there is a 'visceral sense of oneness between their personal self and their group identity'. This level of loyalty has a strength of energy that can propel you and those around you to go to much greater lengths to support other members of the group.

Although you can do plenty by yourself, can you imagine how much you could do when in a group that has the same values, beliefs, drives and vision? Remember, to really propel us to a higher level of success, we need to operate interdependently, not just within the limitations of ourselves!

The challenge lies in having the patience to let loyalty grow, which is understandable given the constant barrage of direct and indirect opportunities to take different paths. Mortgage broker Bernard Desmond is a prime example of how loyalty can catapult your career. Bernard shared on the podcast how he maximises every interaction to build trust, resulting in such deep client loyalty that no one leaves his ecosystem. This has allowed him to build a business in just seven years that could secure his future. Fortunately, Bernard isn't stopping there; he envisions leveraging that loyalty as a solid foundation to build a multi-billion-dollar business.

Another major benefit of loyalty comes when you are loyal to your purpose. To be successful often requires sacrificing things from our lives, which generally comes with a bit of pain. This pain is a reason why many of us don't fulfil our purpose, as it can be daunting. However, instead of focusing on the sacrifice, consider how you are staying loyal to your purpose. For example, you can't lose weight and keep eating donuts at the same time, but I'd argue that the prospect of sacrificing your love of donuts becomes less daunting when you reframe it as remaining loyal to your purpose of losing weight.

It's a subtle but rather substantial rewiring, in that we're swapping something that feels detrimental with something that feels noble and right. Just reflect on that for a moment and consider how cool loyalty could be in your journey towards success.

How much will technology influence our success?

In today's rapidly evolving world, technology has become a significant factor in shaping our paths to success. We can't possibly talk about success without discussing the role that technology is likely to play. I mean, everyone's going mental over the explosion of AI, augmented reality and decentralised currency (crypto, basically), and I'm sure a bunch of you will be eyeing off easier ways to build success for yourself by using technology.

Before I continue, here's a service warning: I'm not going to be giving you in-depth tech advice and crypto strategies! There are people who are a lot more qualified than me to help you navigate the almost 26,000 crypto currencies (according to *Forbes* as of June 2023) and the 79,000 AI companies (as of August 2024 according to Tracxn). What we need to talk about is our mindset around technology, as well as knowing when we're threatening to cross the line from human to commodity.

Is our ability to be human 'crumbling' around us?

I visited a shop in London called Humble Crumble, which offered a straightforward menu of three types of crumble pudding with three different toppings. As I stood at the counter waiting to order, I smiled at one attendant and asked a question of another. When I finally began to place my order, one of the attendants seemed flustered and pointed to a tablet just a few feet away. Although the pudding was delicious, the personal connection was missing. Instead of interacting with the staff, I ended up communicating more with the tablet. This lack of human interaction overshadowed the experience, making me focus more on the staff's unpreparedness for direct engagement. In the end, while the pudding was excellent, the service experience mattered more.

With greater adoption of increasingly common solutions, lots of people and businesses are starting to become rather similar in the way that they operate, heavily relying on their software for a lot of their regular interactions. Aside from that, all these subscriptions and technologies are seriously starting to add up!

According to Statista, the amount of money spent on digital transformation is expected to reach $3.4 trillion worldwide, and Foundry reported that 89% of companies already have a 'digital-first' business strategy. So, it's completely understandable that tech businesses are rushing to milk the insane cash cow with solutions for problems that often don't exist.

The truth is that we're taking on all this technology in some sort of race to be the best in the hope it's going to make us 'different', when in many cases all it's doing is burying the human element in myriad automated emails and AI-written prose. Ironically, we need to become more analytical about our technology choices. Just as we consciously manage our diets to avoid becoming overweight, we should also be mindful to avoid becoming 'tech-obese' by overloading ourselves with too many tools and subscriptions.

Technology is created to make our lives easier, though its rapid growth can sometimes be overwhelming. With AI advancing and technology becoming increasingly integrated, it's true that many human roles could be automated. However, this should not be a source of fear, especially given your curiosity – something that AI can't currently replicate. AI still currently needs information fed into it before it can crack on with its wizardry, so you still absolutely have reasons to be a proud human in a sea of data.

Also, improvements in efficiency should **not** lead to doing less! If a new software saves you time or money, plan how you and/or your team are going to use that saved time. If the amount of pen-pushing is going down, then the amount of human interaction should go up!

The easy way to view and use technology in a healthy way is to apply the Pareto principle, otherwise known as the 80/20 rule. If you were to break down your non-physical functionality (that is, not including physical things like changing your baby's nappy) into its various components, around 80% could be replaced by software and roughly 20% of it still requires your fleshy mind as well as your warm heart. The 80% comprises the pen-pushing, administrative stuff that we generally don't like doing anyway.

From here, we need to use our curiosity to look at the challenges we face regularly and see if we can utilise technology better. Like writing a book... just kidding; as if AI could sound like an English guy this simple!

How do we make the most of technology?

This is not to say that technology is the enemy – far from it – but it does highlight the fact that technology is only going to benefit us if we use the increase in time and money efficiencies to be more human in the way we go about our purpose.

There are a few key habits that I'd recommend when you look at adopting technology to a greater extent:

- **Have a clear, specific goal in mind when adopting a specific technology.** According to a study by Everest Group, 73% of companies fail to gain any business value from their digital transformation because there was no clarity around the desired outcomes from adopting tech changes. If you're taking on a new bit of kit, make sure you set a 'SMART' goal as to how it's going to improve your efforts.

- **Take the time to learn everything about the tech you're plugging into.** Having worked and conversed with several client management systems, the general consensus is that users are lucky if they use 20% of a platform's capabilities. If you're going to buy it, USE IT!

- **If you're in leadership, dedicate time with your team to learn and adopt.** How many times do leaders throw platforms at their staff and expect them to use it when they don't themselves? Your team needs to see you take it on and utilise it before they're going to believe that they should make the effort to learn and utilise it.

- **Find role models that you can follow for advice.** Unless you're planning on working in the tech space full-time, you're simply not going to keep up with the rate of change in the industry. Find someone (or groups of people) that you can hitch your wagon to and learn from. If you try to figure it all out on your own without having some sort of background in it, you'll head down that deep, dark rabbit hole never to be seen again!

Technology is only as good as the amount of effort that you put into understanding it, and when 90% of the world's data was only generated in the last two years, you simply cannot avoid it. Just make sure that you allow technology the time and space for you to become and operate more like a human! In my podcast episode with Jonathan Creek, founder of Virable, he shared how he believes that with the volume of AI-generated content increasing exponentially, the ability to be raw and 'human' will present opportunities for viral content in a sea of engineered 'perfection'. So, make the most of your human imperfections!

> *If you thought there was a lot of content before, there's about to be a shit-tonne more! So the superpower now is going to flip... whoever can be the most human, the most intimate, because robots can't create that!*
>
> *I'm about to start a movement and stamp my content with '100% human'. I'm going the other way man! ... The difference is going to be in the individual creativity that you have as a human.*

Analysis paralysis from information overload

Back in ancient Greece, Seneca was quoted as saying: 'The abundance of books is a distraction', implying that original thought was under threat from the amount of books that were around at the time.

Well, can you imagine what Seneca would say today? Even with the evolution of our brains, there is no way we could possibly process all the information that's thrown around on a daily basis. The University of California San Diego reported that the average American brain consumes around 34 gigabytes of data every day. If we consider how much data is continually being produced, then there's no chance we'll be able to keep up with everything given the limitations of our human computer.

Medical professionals suggest that when we're faced with too much information, it can cloud our judgement, and often lead to anxiety or even depression. This kind of anxiety has also been identified as a symptom of ADHD, indicating that the brain might be struggling to keep up with the information overload. Maybe it's just me, but have you ever felt overwhelmed trying to choose a parking spot in a busy car park? With too many options, I often end up parking as far away from the shop door as possible!

To combat analysis paralysis, focus on simplifying your choices. Set limits on the information you consume and take breaks to clear your mind. By narrowing your focus and making deliberate decisions, you can reduce the feeling of overwhelm and regain control on your path to success.

Will technology and AI take your job?

As the world accelerates through change at a faster rate almost every day, the level to which technology is improving is truly remarkable – and that's an understatement. It can do so much now, and the quality of interaction that AI can have with humans is scarily close to that of a human.

There have been lots of conversations about how tech can and should be used in business, but there is an equal and overwhelming conversation around the roles that technology will take in society and the job market. Large swathes of people are becoming increasingly scared about their job security and even their entire careers.

Now, although I have a degree in engineering, I can't say that I'm the most technologically gifted individual on the planet! I've kind of let my talking do the talking. However, there was a situation I encountered, which split the auctioneering industry, where keeping an open mind around technology benefited me enormously.

Not long after my auction firm had started, a rumour had started that an online auction platform (or two) was being built that was going to change the game forever and potentially take over the way auctions were conducted in Australia. Soon enough, two firms released their platforms, but interestingly, they took different tacks when it came to their integration with the industry:

- Firm A came out with an 'offer management platform', which resembled a more complex and controlled version of eBay, but with the notion that it would integrate as an additional way to sell property alongside auctions.

- Firm B put their flag in the sand and declared: 'Public auctions are dead! This is the way auctions will be conducted from now on'.

Both firms copped a tremendous amount of backlash from several parts of the industry, namely the traditionalists and the closed-minded, which is what I expect a lot of innovators experience.

I met with the founders of both platforms. Of course, I was slightly concerned about what these platforms meant for my beloved craft, but I did think that there could be an opportunity to improve the auction process if the platforms were used in conjunction with a live auction.

The founder from Firm B was very short with his answers and had no interest in engaging with me, but the founder from Firm A was keen to meet up for a coffee and the meeting was wonderfully fruitful. What we ascertained in our conversation was that his platform could serve as the perfect way to reinvigorate a campaign if a property doesn't sell 'under the hammer' at auction, and so we started a collaboration that allowed me to present a full end-to-end auction experience, as opposed to just the call itself.

It gave me a massive advantage, and it only happened because I ran towards the technology to understand whether it could provide me with a competitive edge or an industry improvement before making my judgement on it, rather than running away through fear of the unknown.

Technology is designed to give us more time to be human

Some technology is created to solve problems that don't necessarily exist, but the technology that is here to stay is only designed to do one thing – free us up to become more connected as humans.

I have observed a couple of reasons why there is so much concern around the rate of technological improvement. One is the standard fear of the unknown, but the other cuts a little deeper than that.

Society has become much more reliant on technology than ever before, and until recently it has allowed us to communicate at scale, which makes our communication more efficient but more impersonal as we collect followers rather than friends. However, it's almost like the pendulum is starting to swing back the other way as technology such as AI is creating much greater levels of efficiency to the point that we don't need to communicate at scale anymore. Technology is also effectively forcing us to be more human whether we like it or not. For example, YouTube and other major content platforms now monitor and mark any content that they see has been created or influenced by AI, exposing any content for having a 'robot influence' on it, which is exposing the thing people have forgotten how to do – which is to be human when connecting with their audience!

You need to ask yourself this very important question: What is it that concerns me about technology?

If it's a lack of knowledge, you need to stop being lazy and realise that technology is the key to winning back time for your endeavours. If it's that you're worried AI will take your job, then you need to take a look in the mirror and relearn what it means to be a human, because of all the gifts you have been given, being a human is the greatest one you'll ever get. Technology is designed to help you to enjoy the freedoms that only humans have in this world!

How to satisfy your curiosity for success

We've explored various barriers to achieving your version of success, including defining what that success looks like and creating a path to make it a reality. The remaining sections of this book will guide you further in staying on course and making it happen. However, one crucial element to consider is your belief in your ability to make the necessary changes to move forward.

In 1976, the American psychologist Albert Bandura wrote a review on how 'self-efficacy' (or self-belief) is the core element required for lasting behavioural change. The theory suggests that a person's level of self-efficacy determines how much energy they use in coping with adversity, which then determines whether they have enough energy to sustain themselves through a period of adversity as a behavioural change is initiated.

In a nutshell, the probability of us being able to create any permanent change in our behaviours is determined by the 'expectations of self-efficacy', which is created via four things – performance accomplishments, vicarious experience, verbal persuasion and physiological states:

1. **Performance accomplishments** are the reason celebrating small wins is so important while you go through this process. Marking progress by acknowledging where you've gotten to is vital to reinforce the belief that you can make it to the end goal.

2. **Vicarious experience** is why you need to commit to testing, trying things out and learning by doing. Your mind and body register learning experiences and add those experiences to your vault, which inherently gives you more confidence.

3. **Verbal persuasion** is something I focus on later in Part IV, 'Happiness', but critically, we need to make sure that we are more careful about the information we feed into our minds – the language, commentary and opinions we receive from ourselves as well as others.

4. **Physiological states** refer to the information our senses take in, which implies that our environment plays a big part in our belief in ourselves to get things done. Have you ever had that good feeling that comes from cleaning and organising your desk or room? This is why you feel good about it, because it gives you a greater belief in your ability!

I've touched on all four of these in different ways throughout Part I, but if you go back now and check what you've learned, you'll see for yourself that any action you take from it will contribute towards your self-efficacy or self-belief. As you revisit Part I and continue through the rest of the book, be mindful of any insights you gain in these four areas. Recognising and acknowledging these can significantly boost your self-efficacy, increasing your chances of turning your goals into reality. And the more you do, the more you'll believe that you can actually make this happen!

PART II

INFLUENCE

W hen we talk about the word 'influence' or 'influencer', eyes generally tend to roll. You may immediately think about pretty people who make a perceived mountain of cash by posting photos of themselves perched precariously on a ledge in some luxurious location while pulling off a model pose.

Don't lie – you thought along those lines, right?

The reality is this: influence is everywhere, it's 24/7, and it's largely responsible for shaping our world.

Influence is leadership: it involves guiding others to follow our path, logic or plan. Influence is also authority: when we talk, people listen and remember. It's how ideas grow, movements begin, the world changes and collective identities spread.

We're constantly being influenced, from our environment affecting our energy to parents influencing our worldview and teachers influencing us to reach our potential. Red lights influence us to be more alert, fast-food restaurants make us more hungry by pumping out smells into the street, and Jake Paul influences us to buy an energy drink (produced by a company with a conservative valuation of US$5.5 billion in October 2023) because our kids say it's always on YouTube!

Influence has helped build societies, start wars, amass empires and take down governments. It can hit you between the eyes with a striking billboard or subtly enter your subconscious with a gentle touch on your arm from your partner. Whether we look up to our favourite sports stars or are looked down upon by our bosses, at those in positions of authority over us or those positions that we one day hope to find ourselves in, this will influence our conscience whether we like it or not, from buying decisions to life-defining turns.

It's not all about fake tans, chiselled six-packs (seriously though, they've gotta be drawing some of that shit on!) and some stupid gadget that people get bored with after five minutes. Influence has been, and will forever be, one of the most important capabilities in the world, having an effect on literally everything, everyone and every decision ever made, so it's probably a good idea that we get our shit together with this element of our lives. Quit seeing it through the modern vernacular that has bastardised it and understand that if you want to have **any** degree of success, then understanding how influence works is absolutely vital.

In Part II, you'll gain a greater understanding of what influence is and how it is tied to success, and the different influences that helped to forge your identity (and therefore how you influence others in the same way). I also take a look at more practical things in today's world that hold great influence over society, like technology, media and money.

Questions we'll explore in this part of the book

- Who wants to be an 'influencer'?
- How do you harness your influence?
- Why do you need an online influence?

Chapter 5

Who wants to be an 'influencer'?

*Think twice before you speak, because your words
and influence will plant either the seed of success
or failure in the mind of another.*

Napoleon Hill

Broadly speaking, an influencer is someone who commands enough trust or attachment to influence the decisions, behaviours, feelings and actions of another human.

Influencers can flex their power in many ways. In fact, there are at least 24 different types of influence one person can hold over another according to Google. This is why every moment in our lives has been shaped by some sort of influence, as it can manifest in many different ways.

Guests on my podcast have shared stories about various influences in their lives on their journeys towards success. Regardless of whether the influences were positive or negative, they managed to use them to advance in life. One of the most powerful stories I've heard to date was from Kerryn Harvey, an Australian international para-athlete. After suffering from a rare flesh-eating bacterium, she was hours from death. The immense adversity she faced – barely surviving the infection and losing a shoulder and arm – became a driving force. Despite these challenges, she went on to represent Australia in the World Triathlon Para Championships, making the podium in all but one of the events she competed in.

Kerryn's journey is a powerful testament to the transformative power of influence. In her case, negative influences that came from her circumstances were matched by unwavering influences that came from all of her years training, competing and persisting through pain, culminating in a desire to not only survive the ordeal and subsequent alterations to her life but become a beacon of hope for thousands of others that have suffered life-changing accidents.

The historical importance of influence

It's no coincidence that the most powerful people in world history have been the biggest influencers on societies and communities. Michael H. Hart's book *The 100: A ranking of the most influential persons in history* is thought to have one of the best interpretations of what constitutes influence. Its last edition was published in 1992, so the top ten doesn't include Jake Paul or Taylor Swift (although these guys have scaled their influence better than almost anyone in history), but there are a few names just in the top three that you may be slightly more familiar with:

1. Muhammad (religious leader)
2. Sir Isaac Newton (scientist)
3. Jesus (religious leader)

Just quietly, I think it's fair to say that these three individuals have had – and continue to have – a fair impact on the world. If you look down that list any further, you'll soon realise that influence is the force that moves the world. It's not just a matter of a bit of fruit falling on someone's head, prompting a shout of 'Eureka!' There are key traits that make these figures so influential.

In any area of life throughout modern history, there's someone who has had a major influence, leading to significant changes in how the world thinks and acts. Realistically, any significant change in the world has involved someone with tremendous influence at the forefront, leaving a lasting impact on humanity – whether for good or bad.

Nelson Mandela, for instance, ended apartheid in South Africa and became a global symbol for equal rights. Marie Curie, a two-time Nobel Prize winner, paved the way for women in science with her groundbreaking research around radioactivity and its utilisation in medicine. Leonardo da Vinci led the Renaissance, with his curiosity pushing boundaries in mathematics, philosophy and art and altering the trajectories of these fields. His influence even made a relatively average portrait of Lisa Gherardini one of the most famous paintings in the world – the *Mona Lisa*!

Warren Buffett, the famous investor, is another interesting influencer. His financial prowess is not necessarily his most important influence on the world when compared to the principles and behaviours that got him to the level he's at. 'The Oracle of Omaha' amazes swathes of humans with the simplicity with which he operates his life, forever inspiring millions of people around the world.

What makes someone influential?

I've had some amazing people talk about influence on my podcast, from their own influences to what they believe constitutes influence in general. Maz Farrelly was a TV producer in a previous life, overseeing some of the biggest TV shows in the UK at the time. Maz's take on influence is rather simple:

Everything in life is a TV show … it's your job to make it interesting. When's the last time you went to a meeting and thought: 'I wish that meeting was a bit duller'?

In our conversation, Maz talked about her need to be able to influence the stars (or 'talent') to have them follow direction, which centred around the need to make people feel special and having a bit more fun every day while you do it:

An influencer is someone that others want to listen to … a human that other humans like to follow.

Jon Levy, author of the best-selling book *You're Invited* and founder of high-profile networking program The Influencers, has made the science of influence his life's work and does a bloody good job conveying his findings. Through his observations, Jon discovered four elements of influential humans:

1. **Generosity.** Be giving of your time, knowledge and resources, and give before you ask.
2. **Novelty.** It's important to have similar views to those in your community, but diversity of opinion is just as important.
3. **Curation.** Add value to relevant information by selecting, organising and interpreting it for a community.
4. **Awe.** This is cultivated through the aura of confidence that has people looking at you with their jaws slightly closer to the floor, while making them feel valued in their attention.

If you head to Google, you'll find all sorts of lists about what makes someone influential. Let me throw a bunch of them into a melting pot for you and pick out some that appear more commonly than others:

- **Self-belief.** Influencers have complete belief in who they are and what they stand for. Whether it's a political message, a scientific theory or a Zoolander-esque belief that they're really, really good looking, there is a true north as to what they represent.

- **Integrity.** Whether their beliefs are noble or not, their message remains consistent in everything they say or convey.

- **Ability to communicate.** The difference between the millions of people who have amazing ideas and the few who succeed is the ability to communicate their ideas in a way that is relevant and connects to other people's thoughts and feelings.

- **Self-awareness.** They know what they know, they know what they're good at, and they maximise their strengths while keeping an eye on their weaknesses.

- **They know who their people are.** Every great influencer has a clear understanding of their key audience and knows how to connect with them both individually and at scale.

- **They don't just talk, they DO.** Creating belief with words alone only gets you so far; at some point the audience needs to see proof of concept in order to buy in fully.

- **They think beyond themselves.** The purpose of their existence reaches far beyond their own being, and their vision generally leads to the betterment of their people.

- **They share in the wins and losses.** Influencers aren't glory-hunters! They're prepared to be wrong just as much as right and have no fear of defining their opinions and beliefs in the face of adversity. (For example, a parent makes their child do their homework despite countless protests because the parent **believes** it will help the child in the long term, even if trigonometry is a wonderful life skill that no one ever uses in the real world!)

Influence is a product of self-belief and understanding combined with action and utilised towards a greater purpose. Basically, influence cannot be faked!

What influences different generations?

It's fascinating to see how the world has shaped different generations, and you don't have to dig too deep to understand why. If you look at and pay attention to the major events of the time for each generation, it goes a long way to explaining the importance different generations place on certain values.

Baby boomers (born 1946 to 1964) came into the world right after World War II, during a time when humanity was breathing a collective sigh of relief as society began to return to normality. With a strong focus on working hard to regenerate wealth and prosperity, parents were busy raising kids and providing them with as much as they could. The industrial sector flourished and presented new roles and responsibilities that gave baby boomers new paths for personal growth. This generation thrived on a sense of determination and ambition, often following paths that promised self-improvement. They become very self-focused and began to have much greater levels of independent thinking.

Generation X (born 1965 to 1979) grew up with the anxiety of another potential world war. They also experienced a significant rise in divorce rates during their formative years, which naturally led to a more suspicious and cautious outlook on life. They became focused on self-reliance and struggled to trust their fellow man, so influences that played into self-preservation held appeal.

Generation Y (born 1980 to 1994), commonly known as 'millennials', is the internet generation. They matured as the World Wide Web rapidly expanded, making the world feel smaller and more connected. With the great power that came with having a world of information at their fingertips, Gen Y were let loose on Google before their parents had a chance to realise that much of the content should be reserved for adult eyes. Computer games became central to this generation, and the birth of social media led to Gen Y becoming the most connected and sociable generation to date. Their emphasis on relationships and connectivity also made them more impressionable in many ways.

Generation Z (born 1995 to 2009) has never known a world without the internet. This constant connectivity means their influences are not confined to a specific location – every social issue is fed directly into their minds. This exposure has fuelled a high level of tolerance and diversity within Gen Z, while also making them the most action-oriented generation, though they can be somewhat impatient. The disruptions caused by the COVID-19 pandemic at a really impressionable age have deeply affected them, and the relentless exposure to pessimistic news of wars and world issues (you can't bloody escape it!) has been a significant burden. However, the ease of access to tools and resources means that Gen Z is adept at finding ways to generate income, even in the face of economic uncertainty. Their heightened awareness of social issues drives them towards the loudest voices while also creating a fear of public backlash should they express an opinion that deviates from the voice of the day.

When you take a moment to step back and consider how vastly different the world has been for each generation, the need for distinct approaches when connecting with, let alone influencing, each generation becomes clear. It also makes a bit of a mockery of the constant arguing and finger-pointing between generations when it comes to who has it easier and who has the better attitude/work ethic/[insert any comparative measure here]. The most common argument I hear is the boomers and Gen Xers having a real bee in their bonnet around Gen Z's lack of work ethic and commitment. Gen Z, in turn, argues that older generations simply don't listen.

If meaningful influence is to occur between generations, it must start with empathy – understanding the unique realities and influences that have shaped each generation. I've always said that if Gen X took a look in the mirror and realised that this 'lazy' Gen Z could communicate at scale way quicker than they ever could, then a bit more 'cooperative' influence would result in Gen X being able to extend their earning capacity and level of connection and earn back some time for themselves! And if gen Z took a second to listen to Gen X's knowledge and awareness around key topics, then perhaps they could pick up a couple of shortcuts on their journey towards their ideal life by embracing a degree of 'intellectual' influence!

Who influenced me?

I had a thought about who the biggest influencers were in my life and why they had such an impact. Obviously, our parents have the most impact on our lives, but outside of Kaz (a.k.a. Mum) and Big Jim, my list wasn't quite as extensive as I thought it would be.

Celebrities didn't really resonate with me, but my formative years were before social media (and mostly pre-internet). I had plenty of teachers who helped me on my journey, and whether I liked them or not, they all had a positive influence on me (even if they were being arseholes at the time!). I had one biology teacher who gave me a D on my report card, not because my answers were incorrect but because my handwriting resembled that of a spider crawling across the page, and he embarrassed me in front of the class with it. That was an influence through adversity. I had to prove him wrong, and in the end of year exams, he had no choice but to give me an A because I worked my arse off to ace the thing just to shut him up. When he asked me in front of the class if I was going to consider selecting biology as a subject the next year, I calmly replied that he couldn't pay me enough! Not overly noble, but I just had to!

There were a few more significant events that influenced my life and personality. There was another arsehole, this time in army cadet camp, who taught me the value of standing up for what I believe is right. This old prick was a sergeant major of the British Army who clearly didn't want to be overseeing the rifle range drills of a bunch of 15-year-olds. He was a cantankerous, pompous, archaic individual who was clearly being shuffled out the door.

I was a corporal at the time, which put me in the leadership group at my age level, but aside from that I felt this responsibility to look after my fellow cadets because they were friends or students in my school, so I automatically cared about them. During the briefing, this sergeant major quizzed us about our modified SA80 rifles (they had taken the automatic bit off them).

'What is the range of your modified SA80 cadet rifles?' he asked.

'Range is 500 metres, Sir, with sight adjustments per 100 metres', I replied. (I knew my shit.)

'That's ridiculous, boy, don't be so stupid. These are 10-metre adjustments.'

I bit my tongue even though I knew I was right because I felt that I had to respect his authority. I waited for my Officer in Charge

(OIC) to politely correct him. This guy carried on at all of us like we didn't deserve to be in his presence, and his disdain increased when it came to the girls in my section, with a lot of his energy focused on Annie, who had been dealing with knee problems.

We had to do a 'run and shoot', which is when we sprint 50 metres, drop into a bunker and fire at a target 200 metres away. Annie was really apprehensive, but the sergeant major forced her to take part, and his general attitude started to make my blood boil, which I hadn't experienced before. After the drill, Annie was limping and in tears, and the guy started to gloat at the ease of the exercise and how 'ridiculous' it was of her to be shying away from taking part.

I exploded! 'SHE'S CRYING, MAN, CAN'T YOU SEE?'

A 15-year-old corporal cadet challenging a supposedly decorated sergeant major of the British Army is typically not a great idea.

'How dare you, boy! I will take you around those sheds and give you a good hiding for your insubordination! Never has anyone shown so much disrespect!'

After we were separated, my OIC escorted me away, and I fully expected to get kicked out. That possibility upset me, because I loved being a part of the cadets and the mateship that it created. I didn't get kicked out, but I wasn't allowed back on that rifle range!

This experience unlocked a very powerful part of me that I've been working with ever since. Loyalty is huge for me, and although I had to square up to that hideous human being to find it, I'm really grateful that I did, and I'm grateful for him, too.

Not all influences come from bad things, though! One of my biggest influences was a man aptly named 'The Godfather'! Ian Peake, my neighbour for most of my childhood, called himself a professor at the 'University of Life'. It wasn't just the life skills he taught me that made such an impact, though those were plentiful. Growing up two doors down from him, I learned how to play poker, how to judge the quality of a curry by the sweat it caused and, at around eight years old, which part of the cow was used for fast-food burgers… while I was eating one:

Think about it, And (he always called me 'And'): all the best bits of a cow are used for steaks, the shit fatty bits are used for stews, the ribs are for the barbeque, the brains and eyes are used for delicacies, the tail and bones are used for soup and stuff, we eat the livers and the internal bits, so what's left? The lips and arseholes! Has to be, they're all that's left! Enjoy your burger!

But more than his words, it was the way he carried himself that was the biggest influence on me – and to this day, I still haven't got it totally nailed! His view on people and the world, and how he interacted with others, was so true to who he was and therefore was completely consistent, irrespective of where that person came from, how old they were and what they were about. He had a confidence that commanded respect without being in your face, and a level of observation that made his wit, his responses to questions and his general demeanour one of absolute certainty. The level of inspirational influence he had on me was incredible.

He wasn't called The Godfather just because he smoked cigars and looked like he belonged in *The Sopranos* – his personality epitomised what it takes to be someone whose word is undeniable.

Why do you need to influence others?

Influence is all around us, in everything we do and experience. It's in the conversations you have with the really irritating customer service team on the phone, and it's constantly being projected onto us through branding and advertising. To be honest, it's pretty much impossible **not** to influence people in some way unless you want to live like a hermit! Every action we take, no matter how small, leaves an impact – whether on ourselves or others.

So, it's really not a case of 'needing' to influence people. Believe it or not, you'll already be doing that to those closest to you. Instead, it's about how much influence you want or need to have to achieve what you want in life. It's about understanding the art of influence so that you can maximise the impression you leave on the world and those around you.

That idea might sound overwhelming – leaving an impression on the world. It gives me butterflies just thinking about it. But the reality is that every single one of us leaves an impression when we're gone. Have you ever wondered what yours will be? You're going to leave one, whether you like it or not, so wouldn't you want it to be a positive one?

Now, admittedly, you might not want to have a massive impact that creates seismic shifts in the world, but the person with the greatest impact potential in **your** world is you. Your world includes everything that you love and everyone that you care about, so it stands to reason that you start taking this influence thing very fucking seriously, because your impact is 100% guaranteed to influence the lives of everyone that you care about at the very least, as well as anyone that you want or need to have involved in your journey towards your version of success (and you will need at least some people!). If you don't get this right, the chance of you making any real improvement in your life is negatively impacted, making success that much less likely.

And that's not even the scary bit! Beyond your loved ones, you will influence every single person you come into contact with, whether in a big or small way, positively or negatively. For example, the number of waiters and waitresses I've met along the way who have been negatively influenced by idiots who treated them like shit for no reason is mental. And there's the teacher who told artist Danielle Weber that art will never be a career for her; denying her dreams at a young age actually inspired her to shine. Or consider Javeno McLean, a personal trainer who, at just 16, stood up to adults ignoring a disabled relative during a game of cricket, sparking his lifelong passion for helping the disabled and terminally ill.

Now that we've established how influence shapes our lives and the world around us, it's time to shift our focus to the next crucial step: harnessing our own influence. In the next chapter, I explore practical strategies and insights that will help you take control of your influence, using it intentionally to create the success and impact you desire.

Chapter 6

How do you harness your influence?

*One reason why birds and horses are not unhappy is because
they are not trying to impress other birds and horses.*

Dale Carnegie, *How to Win Friends and Influence People*

When building and mastering any skill, consistency is key, and this comes from discipline or attaching the skill to one's own identity.

I have a famous quote from one of my favourite influencers, American entrepreneur, author and motivational speaker Jim Rohn, ringing in my ears when it comes to this: 'It all matters!' When he talks about discipline, he quite rightly points out that a lack of discipline in one little facet of your life permeates to all the others, as well as how a little improvement in discipline can greatly influence how you roll with everything else.

In terms of influence, the core idea is that the ethos you carry in one aspect of your influence will shape the entirety of your attempt to be influential. It's that classic example of observing how people treat waiters – if it's different to how they're treating you, their inconsistent behaviour indicates a lack of genuine courtesy.

So, how do humans impact each other and themselves? It begins with our belief system. Real, tangible influence begins with the conviction we have in our purpose, intentions, words and actions. Alignment between our beliefs and our actions creates an undeniably genuine level of authentic influence that has way more potential to succeed.

Have you ever felt awkward during a conversation because you weren't sure if what you were saying was legitimate? That awkward feeling is identifying that what you're about to say – or, more importantly, the intention around why you're saying it – is bullshit. You may not mean for it to be, but ultimately, nothing beats the truth.

Elite influencers believe deeply in what they say. If you feel uneasy about presenting an idea, it might not be ready yet, meaning you need to fully commit to it yourself, despite potential consequences.

The key difference between those who succeed and those who don't is belief. Many people have good ideas, but the standout successes are those who truly believe in their idea and themselves, and have the courage to take action based on that belief.

Ways to harness your influence

Let's look at some of the ways you can harness your influence.

Understand your internal communication

Before you can effectively influence others, you must first understand how you are influencing yourself. If you constantly speak negatively or have a pessimistic outlook, this energy will negatively impact your influence and likely affect your audience in an adverse way.

There has been a decent amount of speculative research that points towards a correlation between the tone or vocabulary of our inner voices and the resulting mood it puts us into, which naturally has an influence on those around us. A negative inner voice has also shown to reduce the functionality of our brains with respect to things like memory and learning.

Back in 1934, Russian psychologist Lev Vygotsky developed a model explaining how our 'internal speech' evolves from external dialogue. As children, we often verbalise our thoughts when working through tasks with adults. Over time, this 'external dialogue' becomes internalised, meaning we continue to talk through tasks internally as we mature. This inner dialogue greatly influences our actions – or our enthusiasm towards those actions, at least.

Put it this way: if you think about how you talk to yourself now, would you be worried if you heard a five-year-old kid talking to themselves in the same vein? Chances are you would. This highlights that our internal dialogue shapes how we approach situations, and that we are highly susceptible to what we say to ourselves, whether consciously or unconsciously.

Understanding this, it's clear that you can't effectively influence others without first addressing and improving your internal narrative. As Tony Robbins says: 'The quality of our thoughts affects the quality of our actions'.

Ensure the quality of incoming information

To effectively influence others, you need a steady supply of intellectual fuel from reliable sources. People are looking for you to show them the way, so you need to ensure that not only do you keep sharpening the saw but you also constantly question the current state of affairs.

A 2017 study mapped the level of intelligence against the perceived level of leadership and found that ideal leaders tend to operate with a 20% higher IQ than the average human. To remain an early adopter of knowledge takes some effort to maintain!

Scott Bateman, the founder of Kolmeo, put it very simply on the podcast when he said that he is always curious. Dan White, Executive Director of real estate group Ray White, went one step further, defining the mentality of a successful person by saying that they are 'an expert, but behave like a beginner ... restless for what is possible'.

It's not just about acquiring knowledge; the quality of your interactions also impacts your influence. For instance, empathic individuals, who absorb the emotions of others, can be affected by negative energy from those around them. People with ADHD might also mirror their environment, making it important to be mindful of the information and people you engage with.

Understand the language of your audience

An idea is only effective if you can communicate it clearly. Scientists and tech-heads can really fall foul of this bit because the language that they understand concepts with is likely to be totally different to how it's supposed to be perceived by the end user, and this miscommunication can lead to a disconnect in understanding and value.

In organisations, a 2023 study by Project.co showed that poor or misinterpreted communication in workspaces results in 70% of the audience feeling that their time had been wasted and 55% not even understanding the intended message.

One of Stephen R. Covey's principles in his book *The 7 Habits of Highly Effective People* is to 'seek to understand before being understood'. It emphasises that you have to put time into understanding what makes your audience tick before you can apply your influence effectively.

Ultimately, mastering the art of communication means bridging the gap between your message and your audience, ensuring that your ideas resonate clearly and effectively.

Identify your best method of communication

Various articles and studies have shown that as many as 75% of people have a strong fear of public speaking, and a National Literacy Trust study from the UK showed that the volume of young people who actively write daily almost halved in 2023 alone! But not to worry – effective influence isn't limited to public speaking or writing. Whichever way inclined you may be, there are so many different ways to communicate your influence effectively.

Consider artists. I know a lad who has a relatively poor vocabulary and doesn't do well at school; he is clever in his own head, but articulating it makes him sound a bit stupid. However, put a pencil in his hand and a bit of blank paper in front of him and the power of communication that he has via his art is off the charts! Would I ever put him on stage in front of a group of people? No way! But could he hold influence over a generation if he went all-in with his artwork? Quite possibly. It's a big call, but he is just that good, and his art speaks way better than anything he could say with words.

Don't let the standard way of speaking on a platform put you off believing in your ability to influence. There are millions of examples via the arts that prove influence can be created in any way as long as it allows you to communicate your truth.

On that, understanding your truth well enough to be able to translate it into relatable language is the last piece of this puzzle.

A half-baked idea is not an idea that has been completely thought through, tested for chinks in the armour, simulated internally and fully believed in. Understanding the energy and the intention behind the idea also plays a huge part in how you are received, and that is formed by your truth.

Demonstrate unwavering commitment and consistency

Reliability and dedication will significantly influence your audience intellectually and emotionally.

Another word that describes this is 'predictability'. If you are predictable in your actions, words and behaviours, then the impact of your influence improves dramatically because, put simply, predictability removes anxiety.

Leanne Pilkington, CEO of Laing+Simmons, has garnered tremendous influence over her industry. In her podcast appearance, she described how consistent and committed she is to supporting her people, and her behaviours towards that North Star have led to a lot of people returning the commitment with their loyalty. Her actions in taking on roles such as President of the Real Estate Institute of New South Wales, and now being nominated as the President of the Real Estate Institute of Australia actively demonstrates this level of commitment.

An amazing 2018 study by Bazzi, Ebert, Hogan and Sternad demonstrated that humans crave predictability. The study showed that tasks involving predictable elements, such as the turning of a key or the cracking of a whip, yield better results and lead to stability in our actions, which shows that our brains struggle to process situations that lack a degree of predictability. So, if you want to be successful with people and have their minds open to paying attention to you, then you had better be committed and consistent in your actions!

Remove your ego

If all you worry about is how you look, how you sound and whether people are going to be influenced positively or negatively by you, then your idea will stay in your head and never see the light of day. The ability to take on scrutiny and judgement is imperative for you to hold influence. In fact, you **need** to be judged by others in order to hold any influence at all!

If you're not being judged, then you're not being noticed, which means that your genius idea or concept isn't even being heard in the first place. Get this into your head and you'll go from fearing judgement to almost enjoying it!

How can you transform negative influences into personal growth?

Understanding our past influences plays a key role in influencing our audience moving forward, both positively and negatively. As I've highlighted with a few of my past influences, we can carry that shit with us for a long time unless we identify the need to remove it.

Some people use the past as a driving force, others use it as an excuse to not move forward or evolve because 'that's the way it has always been', and some, well, they just don't register that anything has influenced them at all! If you're reading this scribble of mine then I'm confident you are at least aware of certain influential people or events that have forged you into the person you are today, and that's a start.

Positive influences are fab. They are easy to revisit in your mind and should be reflected upon from time to time to remind us of the good lessons we have learned from them. It's generally the negative influences that are hard to go back to, and to my knowledge, they tend to have a much stronger grip on our behaviours until any issues resulting from them are actively resolved.

Whichever way you chop it up, our negative influences – especially from childhood – play a huge role in our actions towards success, whether it be through behaviours, triggers or something else of that nature. These influences can determine our level of discipline and commitment towards our purpose, as well as causing us to bring in people who aren't aligned with what we want to achieve.

What's fuelling negative influences?

To have an influence is to have an important effect on a person via a strong emotion. This means that missing the bus once may not influence you, but a significant event (or, alternatively, the consistent missing of buses!) most certainly could invoke huge change in your character or behaviour.

The list of poor consequences that negative influences can create is extensive, and they'll make life a little bit more challenging if you want to be successful! Without meaning to rattle your cage, see how many of the following you've experienced:

- Self-doubt
- Low confidence
- Procrastination
- Fear of failure
- Comparison
- Limiting belief systems
- Jealousy.

Don't worry if you've experienced a few of these because we all have. In fact, I'd be shouting 'BINGO!' because I've got all of those ticked off! There are so many traps to fall into when you start to venture forth with your purpose, it's almost like our brains go hunting for them.

Various studies and a good amount of empirical data have shown that our brains prefer to dwell on the negative rather than celebrate success. Kendra Cherry summarises this on Verywell Mind, saying: 'Also known as positive-negative asymmetry, this negativity bias means that we feel the sting of a rebuke more powerfully than we feel the joy of praise'. The brain is designed to be our natural safety mechanism, so when we combine this with the rise in the negative influence of the internet, there's a lot of magnified negativity to focus on, and our brains are drawn to it like a moth to a flame. It's possibly why the news reports are as delightfully optimistic as they are – makes sense when human nature suggests that we're more likely to tune in.

So, if we're drawn to negativity, which has the potential to derail our trip towards success, then how do we go about building a framework that can keep us from falling into that trap? This question ties into a larger discussion around happiness, which I tackle later in the book. For now, it's a good idea to begin to consciously identify when you're experiencing the effects of negative online influence. If you can identify it as it happens, you can become more accurate with strategic thinking around how you can get past, through or over whatever's holding you back. Otherwise, you'll be forever pissing in the wind wondering why you keep being held back by this bullshit – and it is bullshit, by the way!

How do you get over these issues?

The truth of the matter is this: you ain't ever gonna get rid of these consequences completely! Nor should you want to, because then you'll never feel challenged, which makes for a rather boring existence.

One thing I will say is that each one of those consequences can either serve to upset and influence you away from your purpose, or it can be a signal that you need a refinement, upgrade or recalibration of either your education, motivation or purpose.

For example, if you see someone on Instagram who is aiming for a similar goal to yours, your reaction can go one of three ways:

1. You become apprehensive because you think they're better than you.

2. You look at the good and bad, take a chance to see where you could be better and tip your cap to the competition.

3. You use it as fuel and think: 'Fuck you, I'm going to smash it'.

You can't ignore the alarm when it goes off in your head, but if you can become self-aware about comparison being something you may be susceptible to, you have an opportunity to slow the reaction down for a second and make a conscious choice as to how you are going to let the content affect you.

Slowing down a situation and separating emotion from reality can prevent you from falling into all sorts of trouble. Take Kay Bretz, an Australian ultramarathon runner who has tackled races of up to 350 kilometres. He shared a story on my podcast about a race he was leading when he lost his way and ended up disoriented in the bush at night. In that isolated, dark environment, it's easy to understand why he might have felt panic. As his chance of winning faded, his emotions surged. Yet, Kay handled it brilliantly by recognising that his feelings were reactions to the situation, and that the situation itself – being lost in the wilderness – was the real danger. His ability to separate his emotions from the reality of the threat allowed him to manage the crisis effectively.

It's perfectly OK to feel annoyed, worried or anxious about someone else's content or influence. What's important is having the self-control to step back and view the situation objectively. By seeing the full reality, rather than just reacting emotionally, you'll find that many of these concerns become much less significant.

As you can now see, influence is about way more than bikinis and whitened teeth. Influence is the thing that creates action and constantly keeps us on our toes. The way in which we influence, and are being influenced by, people and things around us alters the trajectory of our lives and the lives of anyone who enters our world in any way, big or small.

It stands to reason, then, that we've got to take this influencing shit a lot more seriously than we have! Whatever your success parameters are, at some stage you will need to either influence people already in your ecosystem or take your ideas to the masses in a way that will bring the support you desire and get you closer to your purpose.

Chapter 7

Why do you need an online influence?

If you make customers unhappy in the physical world,
they might tell six friends. If you make customers unhappy
on the Internet, they can each tell 6,000 friends.

Jeff Bezos

Whether you want to make money or start a movement, it's inevitable that your success will (in part) hinge on how you rock and roll online. There's a brilliant statistics website called Statista which shows that as of July 2024 there were 5.45 billion internet users, who had an average daily usage time of 6 hours and 35 minutes. Of that time online, 36.2% was spent on social media. That's a lot of eyeballs spending a lot of time consuming content!

The numbers are undeniable, and just based on those top-level stats, it's obvious that if your version of success includes garnering support for a product, service, patented dance move or whatever, then you're going to need to be able to influence people online somehow.

The great thing about finding success online is that it leaves clear clues, and with the internet at our disposal, it's easier than ever to uncover and follow these clues.

Who first used the internet to 'influence' others?

It's no surprise that bloggers were among the first to harness the power of the internet for influence. But not just any old bloggers; mum-bloggers dominated the early waves of influence with the sharing of war stories and tips that helped their fellow mothers kick on with the bloody tough job of raising kids!

In 2005, the first YouTube video was uploaded, which had everyone watching hours of the most mundane tasks, but they did it because this tapped into our insatiable desire to look through the window of someone else's life, and allowed anyone to have their own 'channel': a significant shift from the traditional TV channels of the past.

While social media connectivity was gaining traction in the background of the video revolution, the first known networking platform, Six Degrees, was created in 1997. It became clear that people were no longer constrained by their locality; they could now tell the entire world what they wanted to say. This ability to control one's own narrative created a new kind of currency – attention – that was previously monopolised by huge firms and is now worth trillions of dollars.

This era marked the commercialisation of influence, evolving from a simple pursuit of attention and loyalty to a measurable and data-driven commodity. With 95% of internet users spending time on social media, according to Statista, it's clear that engaging with this platform is crucial for reaching your audience and advancing your goals.

So, how do you make it happen?

There are two major pitfalls to avoid when building influence online:

1. Focusing on what you think your audience wants instead of your truth and purpose
2. Spreading yourself too thin across multiple platforms.

1. Focusing on what you think your audience wants

What brings this about? The dreaded fear of judgement! We spend too long trying to please the masses and we dilute the original purpose that we set out to realise.

Now, there are external variables, such as income pressures, that can make it difficult to stick to your message, but the ability to stand fast in the face of potential adversity is something that most people struggle to ever achieve.

Sarah Cincotta was subjected to a lot of grief in her field of real estate, some of which came from supposedly influential characters, when she started to remotely whisper her message across social media. As she explained on the podcast, the level of belittling was significant, and it took a lot for her to maintain her trajectory when being told that she effectively had 'no chance' of making it as a coach and trainer in her niche.

Let's face it, anyone who pops their head above the norm might cop a shot or two, but the simple advice is this: you won't know until you give it a go, so give it a consistent go over a decent period of time.

2. Spreading yourself too thin across multiple platforms

Many people attempt to be active on numerous platforms, which can lead to burnout and loss of focus. As PR expert Amanda

Delosa shared in her podcast episode, her clients often spend six figures a month for her team to manage content across various platforms to generate influence and awareness. The good news is, she also emphasised that you don't need to invest that much. However, juggling multiple platforms can become a full-time job, causing you to lose sight of your initial goals. Delosa noted: 'Around the six-month mark, if you are consistent ... you start to feel it. People start to notice you more, more people start reaching out more saying, "Oh, I saw you in this article", and you start to feel more visible'. This highlights the importance of focusing your efforts and maintaining consistency for effective influence and visibility.

I've experienced this firsthand. It's easy to get caught up in the advice from industry leaders like Gary Vaynerchuk, who emphasises the importance of being active on multiple platforms. However, trying to emulate this by spreading ourselves too thin can lead to neglecting essential tasks – like making work calls, booking appointments or generating income – while focusing excessively on creating content for every platform.

Take Amanda's advice at first and give yourself permission to just focus on getting one platform executed properly to begin with. That way, you can build those consistency muscles and get into a flow of content before building on the solid foundation that you've started with.

A show that opened my eyes to online influence

Like many others, I had been grounded by COVID-19 and locked away in my own home by the Dan Andrews government in the Australian state of Victoria. There wasn't a heck of a lot I could do as an auctioneer at the time, but my concern for the greater industry was the lack of connection that was being experienced by people within the real-estate space, who generally need to be around people!

With little thought but a pure belief that it would help, I randomly started a live interview show on Facebook called *The Silver Lining* with the purpose of 'maintaining connection in a disconnected society'.

I prepped guests by simply saying that we were going to have an open chat about life, and the only rule I had was that no agendas were allowed to be pushed. Not only did that create a blank canvas for amazing conversations, but my guests felt relieved that they didn't have to put their professional 'mask' on. It was received so well by the audience that I won an industry award for the part I played in assisting an entire industry – and all from my shed and with very little care paid to my physical appearance!

There are some technical aspects to becoming an influencer online that I can't profess to be an expert in. For example, navigating the forever-shifting algorithms is a full-time occupation, and the various platforms are forever updating, changing and tweaking their user experience. But with all the technical aspects to online influencing, there is still one question that you would do well to ask yourself before you crack on with each piece of content: are you doing this to feed your ego, or to fulfil your purpose?

I know I've fallen foul of doing what I think is going to help build my influence, as opposed to what I feel will bring value to my audience. The challenge with online media, and particularly on social media, is that we can be blinded by bright lights and flashy stuff, which can distract you from your core message amid the overwhelming noise of online media.

How does online influence connect with success?

Aligning your purpose with business success offers clear branding and marketing advantages, with the potential for increased product sales if you master algorithm navigation. *Forbes* reported in 2024 that 26.9% of total business activity is conducted online, highlighting the importance of a strong online presence.

But here's the bit that you need to pay attention to, irrespective of what your purpose may be: all of this online influence work, all the content you put up, helps to build your digital footprint, which is essentially your purpose and DNA. Essentially, your digital footprint is who you are when you are not physically around to engage with those you wish to influence. Whether you like it or not, people will judge you more often based on your digital footprint than who you are in person.

Jonathan Creek, founder of Virable, has spent most of his life studying the science of influence online. In his podcast interview, he highlighted that with the recent exponential growth of AI and its use in creating 'artificial' content, huge opportunities are emerging for those who are willing to present their genuine, human selves. As Creek put it: 'A lot of industries are seeing AI as the shortcut … it's just going to amplify the bad bits'. This emphasises the growing value of authenticity and personal touch in an age increasingly dominated by automated and impersonal content.

It's irrefutable that this digital world is going to have a say in the level of your success, so you had best make sure your digital footprint is influencing people towards you and not away from you!

How can the internet influence you *away* from success?

Online influence isn't just about drawing people towards you; everything you see will be influencing you too!

This is not going to turn into an old man rant where I blame social media for the world's troubles, but there are some statistics that we should pay attention to:

- Of social media users, 58% say social media negatively affects their mental health.

- Of users who spend four or more hours per day on social media, 64% report experiencing depression.

- Seven out of ten social media users blame misinformation and disinformation for being negatively affected.

Clearly, not all that glitters is gold, and however stoic you feel you are, this amount of negativity will get to you at some point in one or more forms. Statistically speaking, the internet has become more negative over time. The publication *Mention* did an analysis of 11 billion mentions online, and negative mentions have more than tripled since 2013. (Must be a lot of whinging Poms like me!) When we do venture forth with our purpose, we can become more acutely aware of the scale of negativity because, naturally, we become more protective of what we're putting out there. That negativity comes in a few different forms, either consciously or subconsciously, and we'd do well to bear them in mind so that we can stop them from infiltrating our mindset.

One of the biggest issues (though they're all big, to be fair!) is comparison, which is an arsehole of a thing and is a primary cause of good people being prevented from bringing their brilliance to the fore.

Sam McLean (my first ever podcast guest!) is the Editor in Chief of *Elite Agent* magazine. She brings so much value with her awareness around AI and media in general. Unfortunately, Sam admitted to finding herself feeling very uncomfortable initially when being interviewed or appearing on stage as a speaker, and that's largely down to the comparisons she makes between herself and some of these flashy, silver-tongued business operators she has been interviewing for the magazine over a number of years. Yet, the value that she brings is far beyond most people who broadcast their opinions and insights.

The reality is that Sam is judged based on her deep understanding of crucial and timely topics, and in these areas, she stands far ahead of the competition. It's easy for those on the sidelines to think, *I could do a much better job*, but to truly grasp the world of influence, you need to shift your perspective. If you can't see beyond your comparisons, you'll struggle to recognise the unique strengths and opportunities that set you apart.

Vanity metrics – society's defining barometer

Remember me saying that we need to remove ego from our decision-making when it comes to influence? Well, unfortunately, online platforms are designed to make our ego perk up and get involved with almost **every** decision we make!

One of the more obvious ways it appeals to our ego is via the vanity metrics that apparently determine the success of any content or information we post online. The number of likes, followers, comments and reposts or reshares holds so much sway on how committed we are to our truth and our purpose that it regularly kills off some great ideas!

Vanity metrics refer to the numbers that appear on social media as interactions with your content or profile. When we put content out there, we often begin with the best of intentions, but because of our naivety we judge the perceived impact of our content by the volume of likes it gets. If a certain type of content doesn't work almost immediately, we'll switch to something else, because instead of trusting our truth we see these numbers as a direct representation of our purpose, and eventually our existence, as we go further down the rabbit hole chasing likes and further away from our original purpose for being on the platform.

If you think that this doesn't apply to you, let's test your behaviour with a quick experiment. Take out your phone out and post something to a page or profile that you have some form of care over (whether it's 'you' or your business page or group). Keep your notifications on. See if you feel a pang of disappointment if you don't get an immediate response. I bet when the first notification pops up, you'll wonder if it's for your recent post. If you haven't already, you'll be itching to check and see who and what the notification is about.

Tap on the notification. You might feel a rush of panic or excitement upon seeing someone has indeed liked your post or – even better –made a comment on it! Assuming it's not your mum saying that you're the best person ever (again), from here you will first check to see if the comment is nice or nasty, and once you've determined that, you'll check to see if you know the person who commented, where they're from, and anything else that may be of interest on their profile (such as if they could be a future customer).

Does that sound in any way familiar? Of course it does. I do exactly the same from time to time! We're all human, and when our social media profiles get attention, it feels like an intrusion into our personal space. This triggers an immediate anxiety until our curiosity is satisfied.

The digital drug that alters our brains

Have you ever found yourself endlessly scrolling through social media, only to look up and realise 45 minutes have passed, and you don't recollect any of what you saw?

This phenomenon is driven by an addictive cycle tied to superficial metrics. Every time we receive a 'like', a small hit of dopamine is released in our brain, making us feel good. This chemical reward encourages us to seek more 'likes', leading us to post content that offers immediate gratification rather than content aligned with our long-term goals and purpose.

Is social media to blame? Not entirely. The problem lies in how we interpret and react to these metrics, which often leads to anxiety and disrupts or stops the flow of creativity towards your purpose.

I know for a fact that if I had stayed the course with my original foray into social media and not become so wrapped up in the opinions of others, I would have been so much further down the track that I'd probably be writing this book from a much more salubrious location! Instead of doing two or three live interviews a week in 2020, I'd have been doing them since 2015 when I originally started to play with the then-new Live feature on Facebook. You can imagine the progress, the content and, therefore, the influence that would have been made in that time.

In fact, in late 2021, I had another awesome reminder to stay the course with this stuff. Of all the places I could have been, I was in the fruit section of my local supermarket having just finished at an auction that I live-streamed that night. I had a mask on (because that was the rule at the time) and was minding my own business when a guy randomly stopped me as I was checking out the oranges.

'Is that you, Andy? Andy Reid the auctioneer?'

'It is, yeah. How are you?' (Cue panic as I rack my brain trying to remember if I had sold this guy's house before!)

'Oh, great, I've watched your auction videos for years on LinkedIn to see how the market is going. They're fantastic.'

We spoke for a little while longer, then went our separate ways. I went to check my notifications to see how often he had indicated his appreciation of my content with a like or a comment – not once! The (very polite and perfectly amicable) bastard had consumed my public content and not once let me know on the platform. How dare he consume the content that I put onto a free platform for the world to see!

Here's my point: to be a successful influencer online, you must always maintain focus on your purpose, not on the metrics, because you simply don't know who you are having an impact on and how many people you have influenced along the way. It shouldn't matter how many people you've managed to influence, either. Your belief in an idea didn't start because you thought it might help a billion people; it started because you had complete faith in the idea and want to know if anyone else was compelled to pick up what you're putting down.

To have influence online is to bring an idea, ethos, personality or product to the world with a 'Godfather-like' level of consistency that makes your purpose, energy and intention undeniable.

PART III

CONNECTION

One of my old mentors, Australian speaker, author and personal development coach Rik Rushton, declared that: 'There are no successful hermits', implying that you can't have real success by yourself. To achieve anything worthwhile, you need to be connected to the world (or with those *in* your world at the very least).

How can we possibly survive, let alone thrive, without connections? How can we operate with purpose if we can't remain connected to the world around us? Connection is incredibly vital for success on many levels, so we need to get across it. A lot of the time, people tend to talk **at** each other to try and win, as opposed to connecting **with** each other to create a greater level of collective success that everyone benefits from.

Connection is the quintessential thing that makes us human. It is the link between two people, things or ideas. It allows us to engage, to feel, to collaborate, and provides the platform for interdependent living that is critical when striving for a higher level of performance.

One of the beautiful things about connection that we underestimate is that there are numerous ways one human can link up with another. Sure, you have obvious methods like a physical connection between two people, but the ability to connect spiritually or intellectually via your values or ambitions is the absolute best. Body language, tonality, even simple gestures like smiles and the internationally recognised thumbs up can provide a tremendously profound moment of connection between two people.

One of my standout attributes as an auctioneer that sets me apart is my ability to make several individual connections at once during a call. A key technique I use is matching the buyer's energy, which is often influenced by their emotional response to money (as discussed in Part I). This skill isn't something I was taught; rather, it's something my parents made me aware of from a very young age, and my awareness has only grown over time.

Another remarkable aspect of human connection is its ability to bridge linguistic, cultural and racial barriers. In Melbourne, a lot of the property-buying population are first-generation immigrants whose first language isn't English, which can make things a little tricky when they are trying to buy a house publicly in front of a bunch of strangers! By sharing an empathetic energy, understanding the gravity of their situation and offering a reassuring smile, I can make a significant difference. I've been told that I have a WeChat following on account of the way that I make Chinese customers feel, despite the fact that I don't speak a word of Mandarin.

It's truly a gift to be able to connect with people from any walk of life and make them feel connected and part of something outside of themselves.

There are a few key areas within the topic of connection that contribute rather heavily towards success:

- **Effective communication.** I've always said that when Donald Trump met Kim Jong Un, the most powerful person in the room was the translator! It's no good striving for anything if you can't communicate it in a way that people can understand! You can try to power on, but it'll get very lonely very quickly if you can't bring others along for the ride. This is a two-way street, too, because communicating is just as much about listening as it is about talking!

- **Networking.** This unlocks doors that you would never be able to get the keys for by yourself! Being able to build strong networks amplifies the level of reach and impact you can have, allowing for scale of influence and acceleration of growth. If you can connect your network with your purpose, then you have the chance to generate a level of support that can have you flying towards what you want to achieve. There are so many avenues for networking, including connecting at conferences, gatherings and on social media. Each platform has a depth of opportunity to catapult you forward.

- **Understanding yourself and others.** Connecting with different perspectives allows for a greater level of collaboration and fosters the interdependent success we seek. To achieve this, we need the support of those we've taken the time to understand, and at some point we must offer our support in return. Genuine empathy stems from a solid connection between people and, once established, creates a level of trust that will continue to contribute to your success.

- **Building relationships.** The strength of any group of people – businesses, social movements, sports teams, families – is based almost entirely on the quality of the relationships within it. Tony Robbins famously said: 'The quality of your life is the quality of your relationships', and Henry Ford said: 'Keeping together is progress. Working together is success'. Having the ability to connect with people comes in very handy if and when you need to drive a win home or avoid a sure-fire defeat!

Questions we'll explore in this part of the book

- Before you connect with other people, how do you connect with yourself?
- How do you connect one-on-one?
- How do you win over a crowd and connect at scale?

Chapter 8

Connect with yourself before you connect with other people

Knowing yourself is the beginning of all wisdom.

Aristotle

Your connection with yourself can certainly be the hardest you'll ever make.

Let's start with a question: can you truly describe yourself to someone with absolute clarity and certainty?

Until I called my very first auction in 2012, I hadn't realised that I didn't know who I was. I had recognised in my past life in hospitality management that I felt at ease when the pressure was on, but I just put that down to me enjoying the pressure of the service. Then, on that fateful Saturday morning, my inner shell was cracked open. It took a while to really break that thing wide open, but in that moment, my eyes were opened to a persona that I hadn't met before.

What did I feel in front of that asbestos-riddled weatherboard property? Connection. Each auction after that helped me get become better acquainted with who I really am. The closer I got, the more passionate I became about discovering more.

I'm not sure there's a tougher challenge in this book than figuring out who you are and being comfortable with it. When you meet someone who nails that, their presence is undeniable; they exude a sense of assurance and calm in everything they do.

What do you need to do to connect with yourself?

Finding your internal connection and aligning it with your pursuit of success can be incredibly challenging. There are countless methods available online, and you likely already know about many of them. However, before diving into these methods, there are three crucial things to address to ensure you're prepared to implement them effectively.

Embrace the uncomfortable

Firstly, get this into your head: if you want to move your life up a notch, you must try (and persist with) stuff that will make you feel like an oddball at first!

I'm very 'normal' in whichever way you choose to measure it. I enjoy sports, gamble socially and love having fun. I like to swear (it's taken all of my being to not riddle this drop of literature with profanity!), and I enjoy chilling out on the couch. However, much like you may be right now, I was not happy with my state of existence. I knew that I was destined to be something more than what I was, and it's likely that itch that has you reading this book in the first place!

Embracing the uncomfortable is often referred to as 'getting out of your comfort zone', which is a well-documented require-ment if you want to make improvements to your life. But it's handy to know why it helps, and the key term to understand here is 'neuroplasticity'. As described in *Psychology Today*, neuroplasticity is the brain's ability to rewire itself in response to new experiences over time. It builds new pathways between nerve cells, which allows us to adapt and get used to new circumstances or actions.

If you don't take the time to maintain your brain's neuro-plasticity, it will become stale and less agile. It's like when you leave Play-Doh out of its container – your brain effectively dries and starts to set. If a brain gets left to dry out – that is, if we don't test it with learning – then it struggles to adapt to any further challenges, which is a huge problem given the pace of change we're faced with daily these days.

When I discovered my passion for auctioneering, I knew that I needed to try things I hadn't done before, and I needed my mind to be open to being challenged. But here's the problem that I faced, which you will absolutely need to get over if you want to make any kind of breakthrough: all of the actions or processes I looked at that could open my mind were things that pretty much no one around me was doing. I had no mates who were auctioneers at the time!

This newfound passion also came with a fear of judgement, which can happen when you consider doing things a little differently. Whether it's judgement from loved ones, friends or, most importantly, yourself, there is this sense of awkwardness that floods your consciousness whenever you consider doing something new.

Now, while the prospect of people watching us and judging can be daunting, I'd argue that our own ego is a much greater contributor to this fear than anything (or anyone) else. Either way, the fix is not to hide away, because that'll follow you wherever you go, so learning to 'step out' the emotions at play and slow down your train of thought is a really handy way to make the fear manageable.

There are loads of different coping mechanisms out there, but mine is to simply close my eyes, take a breath and ask myself: 'What will actually happen if it doesn't work out?' The other thing I've realised is that concern or anxiety can often be reframed as anticipation or excitement. If you're waiting for something incredible to happen, the trick is to use your body to steer those emotions in a positive direction. Simple actions like a smile, straightening your shoulders or clapping your hands can help shift your nervous energy into a more positive frame of mind.

Prioritise yourself

The second challenge is one I still struggle with to this day – the need to put yourself first.

Taking time out of your schedule or away from responsibilities like family can burden you with a disproportionate amount of guilt. I suffer from this almost daily, because who am I to care for myself when I have plenty of other people to care for first?

It's time to face this reality: you are the only person who can make any upgrades to your existence, so if you want to be the best version of yourself for you and your loved ones, you **must** invest time, money and effort into it!

Just like with the oxygen mask on an airplane, if you don't give yourself the chance to breathe, grow and replenish, you won't be as useful or as good a human as you want to be for your loved ones and community. Look at it this way: by not giving yourself some attention, you're giving less of yourself to others, which is more selfish than spending that short amount of time refilling your own reserves. The quicker you accept this, the quicker your life and the lives of those around you will start to improve.

My advice, based on learning from failures of my own, is that before you take on anything new, get the backing and buy-in of the person or people closest to you. A lot of the guilt we feel is completely self-imposed. Our loved ones want us to be the happiest we can be, and we often lose sight of that and invent narratives that are simply not true.

Work hard and smart

Finally, if you want more for yourself, then you need to pay for it with energy and effort.

Put simply: STOP BEING LAZY. No one will just give you access to the next level in life – you have to EARN IT. While there are lots of books and movements that push society towards 'working smarter, not harder', what many people fail to acknowledge is that you need to be working hard in the first place to even think about trying to work smarter! So many people who haven't worked hard to begin with see this narrative and think they can skip the hard bit at the start, which is a fast way to just working less and getting further away from achieving anything!

When Tim Ferriss put out his incredible book, *The 4-hour Work Week*, society did what it always does, which is read the headline and run with it, making its own rose-tinted assumptions about it to suit its own agenda. The reality was that Tim had to work his arse off to be in a position to choose his own narrative. He wasn't just handed success on a plate because he magically came up with a theory that he knew would appeal to the masses, exploiting the inherent 'easy route' nature of people with a bullshit strategy.

The reality is this (and highlight this shit in your notes!): working smarter is NOT a substitute for working harder; it is the process of making more from the hard work that you put into your endeavours. It's like driving a car – your GPS may well be able to plot a quicker path to your destination, but the car still needs you to put the fuel into it to make it go anywhere. Your smarts can plot a quicker path to success, but your effort is still required to get there!

How can you connect with yourself?

Here are some actions you can take (one, some or all) if you want to make and strengthen your connection with yourself.

Meditation

Meditation works for a lot of people, and though the perception around meditation is it's a bit hippy, there is a lot of scientific proof to support its benefits. There are nine types of meditation that are commonly practised, but the premise of all of them is to centre you in the present moment.

Healthline provides a thorough overview of meditation and highlights its key benefits, including stress reduction, anxiety control, improvement of emotional health, increased self-awareness, improved attention span, improved demeanour, reduction in addiction, improved quality of sleep, and reduction in pain, inflammation and blood pressure. The best part is that you don't need equipment to meditate!

Honestly, unless it's active meditation (being present by moving), this is not one my fidgety bum gets on with too well, but the evidence is there in spades to recommend that you make a concerted effort to give it a go. I know that when I have an accountability partner who encourages me, I always feel better.

Journalling

If you're an overthinker then journalling is very, very good. Again, there are lots of ways to do this, but just make sure that you have a format of some description before you start so that you can retrace steps a lot easier when you're reflecting on how far you've come. Much like meditation, the purpose of journalling is to centre yourself in the moment, quieten external noise, celebrate wins and reflect on lessons. But there's another thing with journalling that I find really handy.

Like a computer, our brains tend to work a lot better when we have more memory available on our hard drive, which is referred to as 'working memory'. When you have several thoughts racing through your head, the last thing you want to do is keep them bouncing in there because they take up too much of your working memory. This causes you to get worse at things like solving problems and creative thinking (which includes dreaming, hence why you struggle to sleep when you've got loads going on in your head). By journalling, you are essentially downloading those thoughts from your head, which frees up some of your working memory and allows you to think with a lot greater clarity and reason. The knock-on effect of that is that you'll be less stressed and a lot more aware of possible solutions to whatever challenges you're facing.

Exercise

A clear mind comes from a healthy physical being, and evolving your mind through learning promotes a better outlook on life as well as a greater resilience to challenges such as stress.

It's not like you have to flog yourself, either. The UK Department of Health recommends 30 minutes of exercise a day for five days to significantly improve your mental health as well as your physical fitness. Plus, that's exercise that does **not** require a gym membership to execute effectively, such as walking or housework.

Visualisation

Often associated with sport, visualisation – the practice of playing out or rehearsing future scenarios in your mind – is something that most (if not all) successful people use when preparing for a significant event.

I use visualisation a lot! The purpose of it for me is twofold: first, to get used to the potential emotions and associated pressures, and second, to grow in confidence tactically so that I can handle anything that comes my way. I do it for every auction that I head into, which allows me to sense the pressure if no one bids. It allows me to play out worst-case and best-case scenarios and formulate things that I might say in different situations.

Visualisation effectively programs our bodies and minds to react in the best way possible to situations. Blankert and Hamstra set up an experiment that involved testing 65 tennis players to see how visualisation (or 'imagery' as it can also be known) affects both skill and performance level. Although they didn't find any direct correlation between skill mastery and performance specifically, performance in the set task improved significantly as a result of rich imagery brought via a technique called PETTLEP (physical, environment, task, timing, learning, emotion, perspective) imagery, which is fancy terminology for 'as real as you can possibly imagine something, including what all of the senses would experience'!

Basically, the more vividly you visualise a particular scenario and the success of it, the more likely you'll be to make it happen. It might be worth giving it a crack!

Therapy

You might be running a mile from this one, because the perception is that you need to have something wrong with you to need therapy. Totally understandable, but let me ask you a question: would you rather have a preventative measure or a more costly cure?

The Australian Bureau of Statistics reported that 42.9% of people aged 16 to 85 have experienced a mental disorder, so the need for therapy in many of our lives is somewhat evident. However, therapy is not just there to solve problems; it's there to help us to solve complex issues in our lives that we couldn't possibly solve by ourselves without the help of alternative perspectives.

I've been rubber-stamped with acute depression, anxiety and ADHD (I clearly have it all together!), but what I understood quite quickly is that I needed to treat my brain a lot less like an organ and a lot more like a muscle. I had made the mistake of not addressing concerns or issues, choosing to ignore them because my issue wasn't a broken leg and, therefore, I didn't need a doctor. I nearly paid for that mistake with my life… twice.

Like your muscles, your brain builds resilience when it receives attention and exercise, and as mentioned earlier in the book, it needs to learn things to maintain and improve its neuroplasticity. If you want to build a brain that can take you to a new level of success (because your current one has only gotten you to this point in its current form), then having conversations about your mind with a professional and having your current way of thinking challenged is absolutely necessary. Therapy is simply another form of personal development that not only prevents you from potentially following dark trains of thought, like I did, but is necessary if you want your thinking to better reflect the level of success that you want to achieve. I refer to my sessions as my 'mental personal training', checking in with Dr Marie regularly so that I can bounce thoughts around without any biased retort and with an appropriate and educated number of challenges of my existing thinking.

Set rituals/routines at key points of the day

I'm sure you will have heard the phrase 'an apple a day keeps the doctor away', right? Well, it turns out that the phrase wasn't just about eating a Granny Smith or Pink Lady every day!

An awesome paper written by Arlinghaus and Johnston articulates this brilliantly, saying that having an apple every day delivers a lot more health benefits as a result of the routine of it as opposed to the nutritional value of the apple itself. The need to create routine is vital in maintaining healthy habits because the routine protects the habits required to live a healthy lifestyle.

Routines are proven to help focus the mind and provide stability, acting as an anchor amid chaos. They offer a sense of predictability and control, much like having one hand on the wheel while driving. To make routines effective, ensure they fit within the constraints of your life; for instance, maintaining a one-hour morning ritual may be unrealistic with a baby in the house. Make your routines practical and manageable to improve your chances of sticking with them.

Define your purpose

Just a small note on this one! If you can articulate to yourself why you are putting energy into something, you'll be likely to take more actions towards what you want to achieve. Your reasons may change over time, so it's worth revisiting them.

The book I'd recommend to help you with this is Simon Sinek's *Start with Why*, which provides a stepped process to find your reason for being; there's also an online course that goes with it. You need to take it seriously, because it is an emotional experience if you discover anything meaningful. The first time I did it, I asked my friend Jo to help me (because part of the course asks you to get someone you know and trust that isn't your partner to provide feedback). It dug up some realities that I had been ignoring, which brought up some tears for both of us. However, it helped me define my first true purpose at 33 years old: connecting to inspire action. Not a bad place to start. My purpose has evolved since then, but I've loved having a core purpose to come back to, especially in moments of doubt. Have you got a purpose definition? If you have, reflect on it for ten minutes. If you haven't, that's OK – take this as a sign that you're allowed to have one, you deserve one, and you'll feel empowered once you have one.

*

Have a play around with these ways to connect with yourself, and don't be bashful about it – see what sticks. Remember, none of these are going to work if you only do them once, so maybe trial each one for a couple of weeks to see how connected they make you feel.

My favourite ways, which work in combination with each other, are visualisation and rituals. Despite the volume of auctions I have done, I visualise a number of outcomes and have a ritual before each one that culminates with me letting out a big lungful of air as I cross the threshold of the property I'm about to call the auction for.

If I anticipate every potential outcome of an auction and visualise how it plays out in vivid detail in my mind, I'm never surprised and am always prepared to move forward in whatever direction the auction goes. My ritual allows me to feel fully connected to both myself and the task at hand, and it frees me from any other concerns that I may have, priming my mind and body to be totally present in the moment.

How do values help in your vision for success?

When making any decisions, or processing any information, we all use our values as conscious or subconscious filters. If you're in a corporate role, or if you've read any literature about values, you will likely have an idea of the role that values play – and you may have it wrong, in my humble opinion! The common belief is that performance is evaluated based on these values, and that demonstrating them is key to impress bosses and attract customers. In my view, this perspective is not entirely accurate.

If you have your own values, chances are you may have manufactured them to help 'sell' yourself, almost like they are key features of you as a product. They likely include words like 'integrity', 'authenticity' and 'transparency', or other words that have been completely overused and ruined by the corporate world. They're wonderful values to have, but most people have them because they feel that they **should**, rather than them being real values they **know** they have.

I can say this of course because, as is the case with the rest of this book, I've made this exact mistake! My first set of values when I launched my freelance service in 2017 were 'passion, action, transparency and ambition', which is a fabulous set of values to use to market myself as an auctioneer. It's not like I don't value those things, but for a long time they felt staged, and they never flowed out of me comfortably when I explained them to potential clients.

In comparison, my last sales values were 'integrity, passion, action and commitment', which I clubbed together. Talk about vomit in the mouth; that's got more cheese than the moon!

What you need to understand is that values are not a marketing strategy – they should represent you and your DNA in their truest form. You should be able to show your values to your loved ones, or anyone who knows you, and have them recognise those values in you. Your values are what you see as the most important traits in people and what you see as basic requirements in your life.

As you change, so should your values. In the days after Big Jim passed away, I sat in his spot on the couch at home and, as you do in these situations, I reassessed who I was and what I stood for. I looked at my values from the past three years and finally admitted to myself that they didn't represent who I was but more so what I thought people wanted to hear.

So, I scrapped them and spent hours marinating on the key values that truly defined me at that time. I used a process that originated from the great Gary Keller, a legend in business over in the USA, which was a very simple process of elimination from a large list of value-based words (more than 100 of them, I believe) down to three: connection, fun and simplicity.

The process is relatively simple, but takes a bit of uninterrupted time, a clear mind and an ego-excluded commitment to the discovery of what defines your DNA:

1. Google a 'list of values' and print a copy of whichever one looks the most comprehensive. You want to see at least 100 values listed.

2. Let a loved one know where you're going if required and tell them that you're not going to be contactable for a few hours. Identify a space that makes you feel comfortable. Lots of coaches will say 'go into nature', and if that floats your boat then great, but I'd argue that the right habitat is dependent on the person – I'm a concrete jungle boy, so if it were me, I'd be heading into a space in the city, or to a beach so that I can feel the power of the sea.

3. Turn your tech off (or onto 'Do Not Disturb'). If a bit of music in your ears adds to your comfort, go for it, but try not

to have anything playing with lyrics, and be wary that you might be influenced if the music is attached to a memory.

4. With that huge list of values in front of you, give yourself time to circle or highlight the words that instantly appeal to you.

5. Once you've gone through the list for the first time, give yourself a ten-minute break, then go through the highlighted values in the same way with the aim of cutting about half of them from your remaining list. You'll likely cross off even more items this time because you're delving into your core values and giving yourself the space – and permission – to reflect.

6. Rinse and repeat the exercise until you get down to between three and five values. Take your time with this, as identifying what really matters to you is important and will help you navigate this trip to a higher level in life way more than you realise. If you do this properly, you'll likely discover at least one value you had no idea you had, which is pretty cool!

Even looking at my values now makes me smile, and that's what your values should do to you too! They aren't just words born through necessity or convenience; they are the filters through which you determine how important information is to you. You should have a deep belief in, and understanding of, what each of them means to you.

My values represent my style of auctioneering. I owned them and from there felt so much more powerful in how I presented to both my clients and myself. I felt authentic to who I was and my ideal self, and reading them tuned me back into who I needed to be for the world.

If you don't have values, or you have some but don't get those feelings when you think about them, then I beg you to give yourself permission to do this exercise and find three to five value words that are a true representation of you. After that, road-test them with people you trust to get honest feedback. It'll be worth it, trust me!

Celebrating the good and owning the bad!

Being connected to yourself is important if you want to be able to connect as effectively as possible with others. People have an uncanny ability to smell bullshit – especially if you're working in the service or sales sectors, but in every aspect of life, to be fair. If you want to attain a level of success that is sustainable and built on a solid foundation, being connected to both the good and the bad bits of who you are is not a nice-to-have, it's absolutely necessary.

Believe it or not, the sun doesn't shine out of your bottom, nor mine! But some people clearly think it shines out of theirs, the way that they carry on. Here are a few really important reasons to connect with and take ownership of the less-than-fantastic parts of yourself:

- **Authenticity.** I've tried hard to avoid using this abused and overused word! The simple truth is that authenticity isn't about being happy with who you are; it's about understanding who you aren't and being comfortable with it (but not satisfied, because we're always looking to evolve, right?).

- **Self-awareness.** Talking about understanding who you aren't, if you know and accept your shortcomings then you're in a much better place to identify how you can improve, and your ego won't stand in the way of your progress.

- **Trust.** Owning your vulnerabilities shows that you have nothing to hide, which makes it way easier for people to trust you.

- **Empowerment.** There's a greater level of control and confidence that comes from being connected to all of yourself. It's almost like your collective weaknesses become something of a strength!
- **Reflection.** Reassessing where you're at now gives you a better chance to plot a more accurate path to success moving forward based on your qualities.

Take real estate agents, for example. (Yes, I know, not the most trusted profession ever, but that's why it works to look at them!) One of the biggest parts of the job is listing properties for sale. As part of that process, you are generally invited into a home by the owner for a meeting in which the primary purpose is for you to tell the owner what the property is likely to sell for (based on your experience), what your fees are for selling the property and what you are going to do to sell it to the best of your ability. Most of the time, you'll be pitching for the owner's business against a few competitors who have also been invited at separate times to pitch their ideas around figures and the best plan of attack.

If you win the business, you get the buzz of victory and away you go with it. But if you lose the opportunity, you can go one of two ways with it. It's this reaction that is the biggest indicator of whether the agent is going to be successful in the long term. Most agents' immediate reaction is to find something to blame, such as: 'The other agent told the owner an overinflated sale price' or 'Agent B's commission was so cheap!' It's an automatic reaction to find a reason outside of themselves as to why they lost, and it's a behaviour born from a lack of accountability.

However, for some, the loss becomes a learning experience rather than a setback. Instead of saying that the other agent was cheap, they ask: 'How could I have better demonstrated the added value that justifies my higher commission?' They recognise that the owner chose the service they perceived as right, and the other agent simply operates their business differently. By taking ownership of the loss, they hold themselves accountable and look for ways to improve next time.

If you want to become and stay connected to yourself completely, taking responsibility for setbacks and owning your inadequacies is vital to be connected to the whole you.

In a professional sense, I often suggest that vulnerability is the key to true professionalism. If you know what your shortcomings are and own them, then you will exude the key traits any consumer needs to see. You will be more comfortable being transparent, and operating with genuine integrity becomes way easier. It's the only way to become truly authentic!

Recent studies support the notion that vulnerability unlocks the gate of success in workplaces and teams. Generational shifts have led to a significant increase in comfort expressing and discussing feelings. Today, there is a heightened awareness of gaps in our understanding of personality, though this awareness can sometimes be excessive (but that's a topic for another discussion!).

As discussed in a 2022 *Harvard Business Review* paper, the term 'vulnerability' has been widely misinterpreted within the context of society and the workplace. For many – especially for many men – it's the image of a little baby chick being close to a massive crocodile. This stems from the stoic, masculine 'breadwinner' stereotype. *Show weakness? You've gotta be kidding!*

A lack of vulnerability is like not knowing what lies in the shadows of your own home, in that you know something's there but you're too afraid to investigate. When you think about it, true bravery lies in setting aside your ego and openly communicating what you know and don't know, or what you can and can't do, with your team or counterparts at work. What's more 'manly', if you look at it this way?

This kind of vulnerability demonstrates control and strength far beyond the posturing of those who cannot recognise their own shortcomings. If potential clients or team members see a shortcoming that you don't even acknowledge, what do you think their opinion of you is really going to be?

Without realising all of this, I'd be nowhere near the person I am today; but believe me, it wasn't easy, and it didn't happen overnight. I'm always looking for ways to be better connected to myself, and I still drift away from my values at times, but the growth in awareness alone really does make me feel more comfortable in my own skin, which brings a confidence that attracts new opportunities for success.

The great news is that if you get this stuff above anywhere near right, then your world, along with everything in it, will start to work in flow. Connect with yourself, own who you are, remove your ego and win the freedom to go forth and conquer on a higher level. It takes effort, but my word it is worth it!

What if you lose connection with yourself?

As much as connecting with yourself can improve your level of success, losing that connection can be equally as detrimental to the level of success you ultimately end up achieving. (This applies externally to clients, friends and loved ones as well as with yourself!)

While on this journey to achieving success, we can have our confidence challenged, get hit with imposter syndrome or fall into a deep hole mentally if we're not careful. During that time, it's very easy to lose sight of who we are and the purpose we're connected to. A lot of the time, these are the true tests of how connected you are to yourself and your reason for being. You can get derailed and end up heading in a direction that could cause more harm than good.

There are a couple of ways we can make improvements to mitigate some of the risk of falling into one of these traps.

Examine how you talk to yourself

The way you talk to yourself is the way you define yourself. I think that we are all guilty of not talking positively to ourselves from time to time. Have you ever said things like this to yourself:

> *You are so stupid!*
> *You're so pathetic!*
> *You look so ugly today.*
> *This outfit makes me look so fat.*

I bet you wouldn't talk to your worst enemy the way you talk to yourself at times. We often mutter these comments under our breath, dismissing them as insignificant as we sigh in defeat. The impact of these seemingly small remarks is far greater than we think.

An amazing study was conducted by Ethan Kross in 2014 to test how much self-talk can create or effect anxiety, cross-referencing language with demographics and measuring the level of social anxiety when subjects were put in certain circumstances. The outcomes were profound, with the results even highlighting that talking to yourself in the third person has a positive effect because it detaches you from the emotion to a small degree.

If you define yourself as stupid, then you can study as much as you want but you'll never feel clever! If you define yourself as ugly, then it doesn't matter how much money you throw at surgery, clothes or makeup, you'll always see an ugly reflection in the mirror.

A huge example of this for me was how I treated my success internally. It didn't matter how much I achieved, it was never good or big enough for me to say to myself: 'Andy, that was brilliant, what a huge achievement!' I always played down my wins. Even when I made it to the very top of my chosen craft, I didn't tell myself that I deserved it. In fact, I remember saying to myself: 'It's OK, but I know I could have done better', which is so dumb considering I actually couldn't have at that point!

I want to clarify one thing: you are allowed to always look for ways to improve. It's an incredibly healthy thing to do, so this is not a green light to settle for what you get. But there's no harm in looking back down the mountain to see how far you've come to that point, either. Doing this can help you to stay connected to your purpose, your being and your mission in life.

Avoid changing everything

Like many others, if I lost connection with myself or hit a bad run of form, I wanted things to change immediately, so I went mental with almost any method of reconnection I could find. I'd set mad fitness goals, cut everything out of my diet, start reading a book, change daily routines, write in a journal and become like one of those Buddhist monks all at once, because I wanted my life to change! Each of these methods is perfectly legitimate, I thought, so why not do a bunch of them to get myself back on form ASAP?

As I discovered, this is a recipe for disaster. If you try to change too much at the same time, you're setting yourself ridiculous expectations. Think about it: if you try to make changes to every part of your life at once without being able to change your environment, then how on earth can you expect to have enough energy or mental capacity to make any of those changes stick!

We struggle as it is to spin all our plates in life, and now we want to make them all go quicker at the same time!

This is where I have to tip my cap to James Clear's *Atomic Habits*, the next book I'd recommend that you pick up. The book talks about setting simple triggers to establish habits that lead to a better way of being. It also talks about the importance of 'habit stacking', which is only achievable when done 'one at a time' as opposed to starting five new habits at the same time.

As mentioned earlier in this book, goal setting can be incredibly powerful, especially when paired with the principle of incremental gains – improving by just 1% daily. To build genuine, long-lasting internal confidence, you need to accept that walking comes before running. And that's OK, because we've already discovered the importance and benefits of being connected with ourselves.

Chapter 9

How do you connect one-on-one?

The world belongs to those who set out to conquer it armed with self-confidence and good humour.

Charles Dickens

This entire dance of life is predicated on the dynamics between one human and another. Success revolves around understanding those dynamics and having the ability to make adjustments in character, body language, tonality and demeanour during any interaction.

What I'm about to share could potentially shed a whole different light on how people connect. It seems a bit scientific, and very geeky, but have an open mind as I take you through the dynamics of human interactions and how they contribute to the level of connection between two parties. This has come through a process of me spending countless hours talking to doctors, psychologists and psychiatrists about my own mental health and how I interact with the world.

The line of confidence

The dynamic between two or more people when meeting for the first time (or any time that you're getting to know someone) is often so highly charged with anxiety because of that inherent fear of the unknown. Throw in the expectation of achieving a goal in said meeting (such as winning business, getting a kiss or forging alliances) and the need to build confidence within the context of that dynamic becomes tremendously significant. So, how is the connection between two parties founded? How is it generated to a point where reasonable doubt in an outcome is superseded?

There's a statistical model used in treating psychotherapy patients called a 'normal distribution' or 'Gaussian distribution'. It's used when seeking to understand the probability distribution of a certain outcome, which is helpful given there's never one absolute answer when dealing with the complicated human brain. This model is used right across medicine as well to plot probabilities based on physical attributes.

I've adapted this model to the dynamic between two humans and called it 'the line of confidence'.

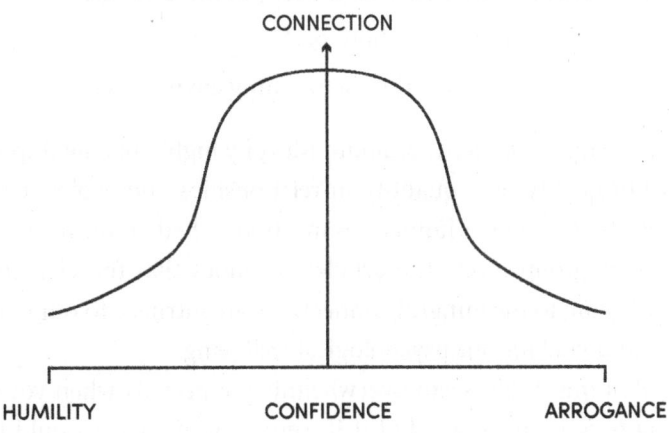

As you can see, at one end of the horizontal axis is humility (or EQ), at the other end is arrogance (or IQ), and confidence sits in the middle.

The vertical axis represents the level of connection (or trust) that two parties feel based on the balance between the EQ and the IQ.

The curve hits low points at the two ends, representing the low probability of connection between two parties based on extreme bias towards acting with humility or arrogance, and reaches peak probability in the centre when all is balanced at a level of confidence.

Here is where it gets interesting (I promise!): a single point on the graph represents the status of the dynamic between the two parties. This point will be in constant motion depending on a number of factors, including:

- what is said, how it is said and how it is received
- body language interpretation
- the level at which information is being received and understood
- the level of presence (concentration) in the dynamic
- the level of relevance for both parties
- the appropriateness of the surrounding environment.

At *Psychology Fanatic*, T. Franklin Murphy highlights the importance of quality over quantity in relationships and explores the factors that enhance human connection, whether on an individual or group level. The article concludes that the elements contributing to meaningful connections are intrinsic to our existence and vital for our psychological wellbeing.

All of this might seem overwhelming, especially when you're trying to win business – but if it were easy, everyone would be doing it, right? Let me break it down to make it more manageable. Put simply, if the total sum of EQ and IQ is balanced, then the probability of creating trust in a fledgling relationship is at a peak.

Let's look at what happens when EQ and IQ are not balanced.

EQ biased

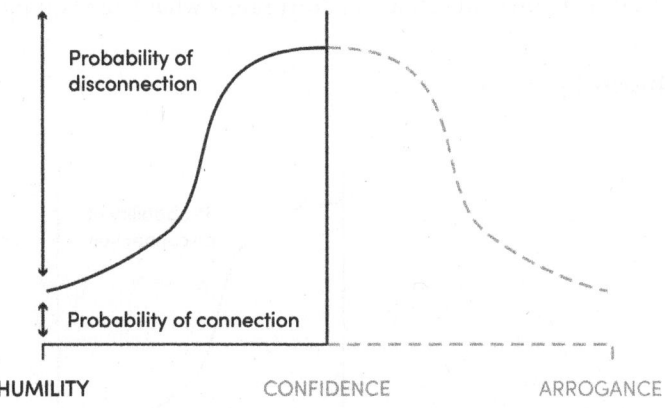

If you have an EQ bias, your business ethos is all about 'making friends with clients and doing what they think is right for them'. This is where I started my professional life! You guys are the warm and fuzzy ones who spend your time drinking tea and talking about the past. Your interest is purely in helping clients, and heaven forbid you should disagree with anything the customer has to say.

This end of the scale makes you feel good at the time, but seldom does it actually translate to a positive outcome in the end. You hear things like: 'We really liked you, but...', or: 'You're a great guy, and if it doesn't work out, you'll be the next person we call', or the dreaded 'friend zone': 'You know, I really enjoy spending time with you, but I just don't want to risk our friendship'.

This is where 'nice people' tend to reside with their inter-actions, which is a really harsh thing to say, but having spent way too long being a nice guy myself, it just doesn't work out well in the long run!

The problem at this end of the scale is a lack of credibility. You can make as much of an EQ connection as possible, but without creating an IQ balance in the relationship, the customer is going to think that you're nice but you don't know what you're doing.

IQ biased

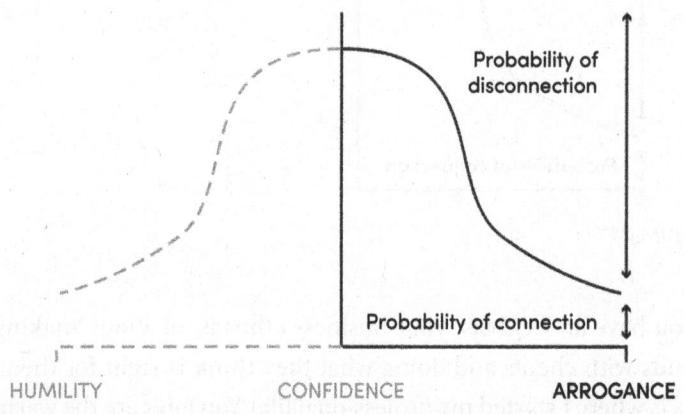

HUMILITY   CONFIDENCE   **ARROGANCE**

If you have an IQ bias, you know what's right for them – the end! A lot of salespeople tend to sit in this category, and that comes down to the way they are trained. Sure, you can convince the occasional person to sign on with you based on a well-rehearsed script, but the minute someone asks you a question beyond that, you're in trouble.

It's all well and good thinking that you know what's best for a customer, but until you can create an EQ balance that makes them feel heard, then you can all but kiss your chances of success goodbye!

The problem that is created at this end of the scale is a lack of understanding. Customers aren't made to feel like they are a part of their own process, or whoever you're dating feels like you don't care about them, even if you can brag about all the stuff you have! Bragging gets you nowhere with most humans, so if you want to improve your probability of building confidence and trust in a dynamic then you might want to reconsider your approach.

How do you achieve connection (and trust) between two unknown parties?

Before we begin, let's make one thing perfectly clear: you are not going to build trust with absolutely everyone! There are over 8 billion people on the planet, all wired differently, so let's be real here and accept that you are simply not destined to get on with some people.

With that being said, there are a number of things you can do and be aware of to increase the probability of building that trust. I'm going to switch purely into business mode here, but it's easy enough to apply these principles to different facets of your life.

Let's very quickly burst the bubble of any arrogant types! There's no way you know more than the internet about anything, and therefore your potential customer can potentially know more than you. Yes, you may be able to talk in generalities to a greater extent, but your customer only cares about the specifics of their situation and will likely have googled more specific information that is relevant to them. However, this is **not** a signal for you to assume their intelligence either! So, clarify their depth of understanding before you go waffling on with what you have to say. If you don't, you may get caught out!

Always set expectations – and meet them

Meeting expectations is huge, especially in initial interactions. The fear of the unknown causes a height of anxiety that clouds judgement. We know that humans are naturally suspicious about anyone they don't know, and yet, when we first meet people, we tend to insist on this dance of trying to work out what the other side wants. In sales, this usually means jumping straight into the presentation because that's what we're there to do.

The issue is that anxiety raises defences, making it almost impossible to connect or communicate effectively.

So, what's the antidote? If fear of the unknown is causing this major barrier, then the solution is to make things known – and quickly – if you want the interaction to head in the right direction.

The easiest way to break down how to achieve this is with three words: intention, detail and agreement. At the beginning of any interaction between unfamiliar parties, taking the initiative to outline a common ground or goal, however big or small, as well as provide a road map on how to achieve it and seek the other party's approval, makes everything about the interaction clear.

How do you think that is going to make the other party feel? It's likely that they'll be a damn sight more relaxed about the time they're about to spend, because you've removed the natural fear that causes the fight-or-flight response in people. It also shows a level of control over your actions, which is always reassuring for people.

While many businesses send out information prior to a work meeting, a piece of paper or an email can't entirely remove that underlying anxiety. You'll recognise these three simple steps in action when surgeons come into the room to explain a procedure.

That's because going under the knife is bloody scary, so they must paint a picture of control and reassure you that you'll be safe in their hands.

Once you've set the expectations of the meeting, make sure to deliver on them! By setting clear expectations, you're creating an opportunity to prove that you do what you say you're going to do, which will build trust with the other party in any aspect of life.

Ask more questions and confirm your understanding

There's no chance of getting past the metaphorical (or literal) front door of a potential customer unless they feel comfortable that you understand the circumstances that lead to a change or purchase being made.

This is where IQ-biased operators tend to fall early on in the interaction, mainly because they're far more focused on being heard than listening! However, many tend to trip over here because they don't feel like they can ask enough questions to get all the necessary information.

My old mentor Rik Rushton, a man who made up for a lack of vertical prowess with a height of intellect, coined the following phrase: 'Tune in before you broadcast'. It's a wonderful metaphor to describe what needs to happen to get on the same wavelength as your potential customer, because you need to ensure you're on the right frequency for your signal to be received.

But asking simple questions isn't enough anymore to reach the level of understanding that customers expect these days. The basics might work for fast-food drive-throughs where kids ask standard questions due to the volume of choices, but if you want to build trust, you need to go beyond that.

Your goal should be to ask an initial question, then follow it up with a secondary question based on the answer you receive.

Why is this important? Because it demonstrates to your potential customer that you're genuinely paying attention to them – not just listening but actively processing their response. The simple act of reconfirming the received information affirms to everyone that the information is both received and understood.

Be present now to keep yourself in their future!

Have you ever tried to talk to someone while they're fidgeting with their pen, looking past you or constantly checking their phone or watch? How does that make you feel when it happens?

I'm sure that you will have heard that body language makes up 93% of our communication. (If not, you have now!) In this context, we need to communicate with our bodies that we are present in the moment. While many sales books from the 1990s recommend 'mirroring' the body language of the other party, I'd argue that this would be highly detrimental if the language that you're mirroring doesn't come naturally to you. In fact, if someone did that to me, I'd instantly think they were mocking me! Plus, focusing too much on mirroring can distract you from actually listening to what the other party has to say.

Being present is not easy these days with the volume of notifications, pings, bings and buzzes that are happening around us, so if you really want to stay present then turn all your tech off! Or at least put it on 'Do Not Disturb', because checking who's calling during a meeting is not ideal. (Note: If you have family members you are responsible for, then of course you can't ignore them, but let the other side know in advance that you may need to pick up the phone if family calls.)

Make eye contact (but not in a creepy way!)

When someone is looking at you and conveying information that is relevant to the potential outcome, that would be a good time to keep locked onto those baby blues so the other person feels like you're fully tuned in.

Oddly, the science of eye contact hasn't been dug into all that much due to technological limitations within brain analysis, but early research has shown physiological changes in pupil dilation, and Yale School of Medicine professor Joy Hirsch (who founded its 'Brain Function Laboratory') has discovered early signs of 'brain synchronicity' between humans when making prolonged eye contact.

Although social studies have estimated that anything longer than four seconds makes things tremendously awkward, the power in communicating your attention level to someone you're interacting with by locking eyes is significant (and becoming scientifically justified).

For goodness sake, though, don't just gaze into their eyes while nothing is being said, because unless fireworks are going off and you're falling madly in love, it's just weird!

Check the tone and speed of your delivery

The tone and speed of your delivery is one area in which I do believe mirroring comes in handy. Being loud and obnoxious to a lovely old lady can be somewhat detrimental, and going in soft with an alpha male is not going to win you any favours!

When you converse, it's so important to be able to match the tone, modality and speed of your communication within reason. It all counts towards tuning into the energy of the other person, and they need to **feel** a degree of commonality to feel comfortable.

In his book *The Relationship Cure*, Dr John Gottman explains that although only 7% of our communication is done through the words we speak, a substantial 38% of our communication is conveyed by the tone of our delivery. Have you ever tried reading a sports report or a horror novel to a baby in a soft, calm tone?

Even if the kid loves their sport, you'll still have them fast asleep in no time at all!

Now, a couple of warnings with this one. Like mirroring in the old-school sense, if playing with tone doesn't come naturally to you then you will get found out, partly because you're likely to sound like a bit of a nutter to them! It's also important to make sure you don't stereotype how people like to be communicated with, because assumptions can bite you on the bum too. I'll never forget 91-year-old Joan Renzow, whose fragile little frame disguised one of the sharpest wits I've ever met to this day. In my first meeting with her she had me running for the hills with my tail between my legs. So, even if you think you know, you really don't sometimes!

Challenge opinions, but provide the intention

People know when you're arguing for the sake of it. Likewise, they know when you're trying to help. They also know when you're being a lapdog and just agreeing to everything, so you need to make sure that the dynamic is one of collaboration.

To do this, you're going to need to be able to show that you're processing opinions, as discussed, but also back your knowledge. Sometimes this can be tricky. For example, if you're dealing with a headstrong individual (high up on the arrogant end of the scale), then expressing a difference of opinion or correcting information is sometimes fraught with danger. However, it can be argued that genuine trust needs to have credibility built into its foundation if the connection is going to be productive and successful. To progress towards any collective success, there needs to be an openness to challenging thoughts.

If you find this difficult then the easy way to start is to under-pin any difference of opinion with a layer of logic. Logic cannot be argued with – a fact is a fact and numbers don't lie. If you know your job well enough (which you do now because we've eradicated excuses already!), then being able to make summations based on logic will be a massive strength for you when earning that credibility. After all, trust is built when there is an exchange of knowledge, not when it's one-way traffic!

Chapter 10

How do you win over a crowd and connect at scale?

Effective communication is 20% what you know and 80% how you feel about what you know.

Jim Rohn

Welcome to my world! If you have any ambition of having your success create a decent impact on your community, your customers or your colleagues and counterparts, then you need to understand how you connect with groups of people.

When you read 'connecting at scale', what immediately springs to mind? Is it social media? Emailing your database? Or perhaps creating videos, podcasts or blogs? Maybe it's the dreaded public speaking, which ranks #2 on the list of things people fear the most.

The challenge isn't just engaging in these activities; it's doing them with a set purpose. Here are the keys to connecting at scale that you always need to be mindful of:

- **Communicate purposefully.** 'Just touching base' with your people is about the most mundane and pointless thing you could do and provides no reason for anyone to engage with you. If you reach out to people, have a proper reason of value! Anything you send needs to have some degree of relevance to its recipient.

- **Make it easier by making it about them.** Having a constant focus on your audience does two things: it makes your people feel like you're paying attention, which earns a bit of trust, and it also removes your ego from the equation. I genuinely feel like the least important person during an auction, despite being the centre of everyone's focus in front of a house!

- **Take ownership of what makes you unique.** There's only one of you, and groups of people will know if you're trying to be something that you're not, so being able to translate who you really are to people is absolutely vital.

- **Accelerate the scale of your impact.** Want to work smarter? Mastering how to scale your voice and your purpose is a primary way to do it, which is hard if you're new to understanding your reason for being. We can't change the world in one go, but we can change one person's world, and if we can improve the rate at which we do that then our goals and purpose will have a better chance of becoming a reality.

When I'm engaging a crowd in front of a property, I have to make two types of connections. The first is with the crowd in its entirety, and the second is on a one-on-one basis with individuals in the crowd to gain that extra degree of familiarity for when the bidding begins.

Depending on the size of the crowd, the energy and the environment, I need to calibrate my scaled connection (the one with the whole group) to suit. Likewise, I need to identify the key individuals and their energy and awareness quickly so I can create a flow of energy on an individual basis that will serve us well. It's one of the most fascinating parts of the craft of auctioneering.

If you have any aspirations or need to connect with lots of people as a part of your passion or purpose, then before you can start to entertain the methods for doing this, you need a fundamental understanding of the core principles that will give you a much better chance of success. Without them, you are simply wasting your time!

A spectacularly bad example of connection!

I spent my senior school years in Nottingham, England, the legendary home of Robin Hood and the infamous Sheriff of Nottingham. So, when I was booked to conduct an auction on Nottingham Street in Glen Waverley, Victoria, a wave of nostalgia washed over me. I couldn't help myself, I crafted the most impressive script for a property auction ever! I included lines like:

- 'Plenty of space under the pergola for your Merry Men to regale you with their tales of triumph!'
- 'Treat your Maid Marion to breakfast at the cafe just around the corner.'
- 'Not even the Sheriff of Nottingham on horseback could infiltrate the security within this home.'
- 'Enough space in your backyard for your very own Sherwood Forest, or at least a miniature version of Trent Bridge for the summer series of cricket!'

Referencing elements of Nottingham in almost every line, it was a poetic masterpiece that even Shakespeare would have been proud of… or so I thought. I delivered my genius script with tone, enthusiasm, energy and drama, thinking: 'I've got these guys in the palm of my hand!' I was smashing it. I delivered my final line with gusto, expecting roses to be thrown from the crowd, tears of joy, and a flood of bidding due to the tremendous anticipation I had built.

Nothing. Not even a smile! The best I got was a cough from someone.

One problem that I hadn't quite accounted for, and had lost sight of in my nostalgic reverie, was the crowd's origin. Hint: not one of them was from England, and they may not have even heard of Robin Hood! Needless to say, the auction bidding took a little longer to get going, but we achieved an amazing outcome in the end. It was a humbling reminder for me that connection requires two parties, not just one with his fanciful ode to his hometown!

What do you focus on first?

There are all sorts of mediums you can use to attempt to connect with large groups of people these days. There are so many platforms, in fact, that many people ask: 'What's the best platform?' before they even think about the message that they want to share. The confusion surrounding the delivery of the message is taking people away from the message, which is way more important when it comes to winning over your audience.

Media expert Immy Callister discussed this with me on the podcast. Many people jump into new platforms or methods simply because they see them online, without evaluating whether these tools actually fit with their existing toolkit or personal style. It's important to consider if a new strategy or platform aligns with what you already have and reflects your personality before adopting it.

Let me ask you this: when you decide to go on a trip, do you decide on the destination first or the method of travel? I mean, sure, if you are a caravaner (which you can clearly tell I am not) then you may have a predetermined mode of transportation in mind, but it's not like you're just taking it out and driving around aimlessly! First, you pick the destination, then you work out how you'll get there. Likewise, when it comes to connecting at scale, you first need to determine where you want to take your audience (metaphorically speaking) before you decide how you're going to get them there.

You don't decide: 'Right, I am going to send an email... what shall I write?'! If that's your approach, you won't have anything meaningful to say, which brings your intention into question.

What and who are you in this for?

There's a reason why people in certain job roles are, on the whole, not trusted. You know that internal alarm system that I talked about earlier? Well, there's another aspect to it that humans use on a daily basis – the bullshit radar!

It really doesn't matter which medium you use to get your message out there until you understand what your intentions are and believe in them. If your purpose is wholly altruistic towards your chosen tribe then great, but if you're in it to make money and provide for your family then that's fine too – just don't try to fool anyone into thinking you're there for them! Whoever you're broadcasting to will be able to pick up on whether you are saying things for their benefit or for your own gain. Depending on the immediacy of any decisions that need to be made, you can burn bridges very quickly if you get this wrong.

It basically boils down to this one question that you need to ask yourself before you broadcast anything: 'Is what I'm about to put out there for my benefit, or my audience's?' If it's for your benefit, don't expect many people to reach out with open arms. However, if you genuinely want to help and have your customers front and centre in all your thoughts, then the energy that comes along with that is undeniable.

Understand what makes you different

You may have heard of unique selling points (USPs). So many people in sales roles ask me how to differentiate themselves from their competitors, and a lot of the time they try to tell me what their business does, how much better their brand is or list other material things they try to sell as significantly better.

With the ease of access to technology, the increasingly cost-effective nature of offshore outsourcing and the capability that we all have in the palm of our hands these days (through our phones), it's really difficult to convince a consumer that they are any better off with brand A than brand B given how similar they are likely to be.

The question is: 'Do you know what your USPs are?'

Oana Aurora wrote a fabulous article about this on *Medium* with five steps for determining your USPs, including showing the other party some of your personality. The confidence that grows from recognising and owning your USPs is a wonderful side-benefit too, so it's worth running the exercise and finding out.

I can honestly say (and get told regularly) that my auction style is very different to that of any other auctioneer for a number of reasons. My accent is markedly different. I'm tall but only throw my chest out when required. I'm not afraid to have spontaneous fun with bidders and agents. I smile! I prepare more than the vast majority, but my personality is dialled up so that people feel and hear more than a scripted auction call. Does it have anything to do with the mechanics of the transaction? No, because the legislation is the same for all of us. Are the tools available any different? Not in the main, although I have a solid level of projection developed from years in acting classes. What's the one true difference I have? It's me! And this is what really needs to be drilled into your head if you want to allow people the chance to connect with you.

What makes you special?

Have you ever heard the saying: 'Comparison is the thief of joy'? Teddy Roosevelt, the 26th President of the United States, is one of many who this saying has been attributed to. Comparison is what prevents so many people in the world from even attempting to make improvements in their lives, and if you're honest, I bet you're doing it to an extent too.

But let's not point fingers at social media for all our problems. Comparison has been a part of human nature since the days when cavemen competed over cave sizes and tried to compensate for their phallic inadequacies with oversized clubs. However, in today's world it has become much easier to compare ourselves to others, with the entire world seemingly in the palm of our hand, showing us what we 'could' have achieved.

Here's what's undeniably true: there is, and will only ever be, one you. Neurologically speaking, it is impossible for another human being to share your exact mental wiring, making you a truly unique specimen. The same goes for our physical makeup – it is literally impossible for anyone to have the same cellular structure. How cool is that?

Yet, acknowledging this fact is easier than truly believing it to be the case. So, how do you get there?

If you head over to the final part of this book – 'Happiness' – you'll find some ideas for how you can define who **you** are in a way that provides you with a true sense of ownership. But in the context of this section of the book, let me illustrate what I mean with a simple example.

Take the colour blue. There are countless shades of blue, each with a fancy name that often baffles the average person. But your interpretation of any shade of blue will never be the same as mine. Why? Without going into the specific science of it, our interpretation of colour and the signals that we send to our brain are defined by the number of cone cells that our retinas have. Depending on how many we have, we see and interpret colours in entirely different ways, which makes it nearly impossible for me to see the exact same blue as you. Interestingly, women tend to have one more set of these cells, meaning they perceive more colours than us men!

There are numerous scientific reasons that prove you are a one-of-a-kind masterpiece, even before we touch on psychological parameters. Ultimately, the quicker you accept this, the more your life and the lives of those around you will start to align with your grand vision. You'll naturally gravitate towards what you want in life. Plus, accepting this within yourself makes it so much easier for others to accept you for who you are, which is a trait I've noticed in every one of my guests on the podcast to date, so there must be something to it!

I know this section got a bit scientific in places; I'm not going to lie, my inner geek had a field day! The sheer volume of factual evidence and scientific research that has been conducted (and in some cases has only just started!) shows that connecting with yourself, and growing that connection with those around you, isn't just desirable – it's essential.

You cannot possibly contemplate success at any level if you're not willing to put the time into this part of your life. For so many, this is the biggest barrier to forging a life of success. Even for those who are logical and less emotional, it's clear that embracing this part of your journey is essential. It's key to bringing your ideas to life, realising your ideals and reaching the full potential you were born with.

PART IV

HAPPINESS

When we glorify the traditional idea of success, it's easy to conclude that the pot of gold is at the end of a rainbow, found by busting your arse in the incessant pursuit of an elusive level of success.

If you were to google the definition of success, you'd find words and phrases like 'persistence' and 'hard work', and the idea that success is a journey rather than a destination. Many wise people suggest that success is achieved through sheer endurance, with little mention of happiness, which makes you wonder: does success alone bring the happiness that makes it all worthwhile?

The argument often made is that success brings the things that make us happy. For example, if a job pays well enough for you to afford a house, car and holidays, then it's worth doing. Some people can compartmentalise their lives this way and make peace with their apathy or disdain for a job if it supplies the money required to fund things outside of work. But it begs the question: how long can we realistically sustain this, especially considering how much of our lives we spend at work?

You don't have to look too hard to find evidence that a singular, intense focus on success can actually lead you **away** from happiness. Many successful actors, sports stars, pop icons and celebrities have struggled with severe depression, anxiety and addictions of various kinds. A 2008 study review by Jayne Barnard from the University of Cincinnati found that CEOs are twice as likely to develop depression due to the intensity of their roles, citing their need to 'escape' their high-pressure situation with something that is equally as intense, such as drugs, adultery, high-octane activities or even creating a secondary existence.

A common trait among many of these 'successful' people is their 'at all costs' mindset towards achievement. Their focus is incredible (something I sometimes envy), but their neglect of other aspects of life often leaves a trail of destruction in their family or personal lives. However, despite the various publicised dramas and failed marriages, the narrative still tends to focus on their success in their chosen field, leaving people like you and me in awe of their achievements.

But what if we looked at it the other way around? What if happiness were considered a critical pillar for long-term, sustainable success?

The idea that happiness could lead to success challenges the standard rhetoric, but it's something the world is waking up to, with a growing number of studies showing that happiness actively improves performance.

One of the most compelling studies I've found involved nearly 1 million soldiers in the US Armed Forces. 'Happy soldiers are highest performers' was a 2021 study that measured positivity, negativity and optimism across a diverse range of soldiers over a four-year period, and predicted and tracked their ability to perform their roles. The results were striking: soldiers with high positivity performed better and earned more awards than those with a negative mindset. In fact, the positive group was four times more likely to win awards for things like heroism and performance, a prediction made with remarkable accuracy.

We've already established that making money is something we all need to get more comfortable with, and there are practical realities to consider – bills still need to be paid, after all! However, the belief that success automatically leads to happiness is a misconception that has left many people feeling unfulfilled despite owning flashy cars and expensive watches.

With that in mind, it's worth pausing to reflect on what truly makes you happy before we dive into this exploration of success.

Questions we'll explore in this final part of the book

- What defines happiness for you?
- What can you do when imposter syndrome gets in the way of happiness and success?
- What happens when the shit hits the fan?

Chapter 11

What defines happiness for you?

Very little is needed to make a happy life.

Marcus Aurelius

Happiness is a concept that has been explored and defined by countless literary works, philosophers and leaders throughout history. Yet, happiness is a deeply personal experience that manifests in all sorts of different forms, shaped by the unique circumstances that trigger those fabulous happy chemicals in your brain.

Many factors influence our happiness – personal connections, work life, social media exposure and the overwhelming flood of content we consume daily. A Harvard study that began in 1938, led by renowned researcher Robert Waldinger, tracked the lives of 725 men and their families and revealed that our relationships and how we nurture them, along with our health, are the biggest influences on our happiness.

Throughout my podcast, my guests have shared their under-standing of what brings them happiness, often discussing their unique paths to success and high performance. For instance, best-selling author and speaker Chris Helder discussed his use of 'useful beliefs' to reshape his perspective on life events, turning challenges into positive experiences and creating clarity to move forward. His episode offers a valuable perspective shift and framework for reframing your approach to happiness and is well worth a listen.

Much like success, I think happiness leaves clues. To help you define what happiness means for you, let's take a look at different types of happiness and build a foundational understanding before we kick on.

What types of happiness are there?

Across many philosophical traditions, happiness is generally divided into two main categories: short-term pleasure and long-lasting, deeper wellbeing.

Hedonic happiness

Hedonic happiness is about seeking immediate, often fleeting, moments of joy. It's the rush of euphoria that comes from endorphins flooding your brain – whether from excitement, joy or laughter. Hedonic happiness is great for lifting your spirits, tackling grief or boredom, and avoiding pain or anxiety.

However, hedonic happiness needs to come with a warning: if pursued excessively, it can lead to a disconnect from reality or a lack of deeper contentment. The pursuit of this immediate relief can sometimes result in unhealthy addictions, such as drugs or alcohol, as people seek to fill voids in their lives. Yet, this same pursuit can also motivate positive changes, like developing a love for exercise or strengthening connections with loved ones.

Eudemonic happiness

Originating from Plato's *Ethics*, eudemonic happiness is about pursuing our highest potential and living with purpose and integrity. It's about finding genuine meaning in life through the constant search for your highest being, which allows you to live more in the present. Each day feels purposeful, driving you to seek progress and ultimately leading to lasting satisfaction. This is why many of my podcast guests have mentioned curiosity as a key mindset for self-improvement. While eudemonic happiness is often seen as superior in moral value, it's important to remember that we are human and need a balance of both types of happiness in our daily lives. Incorporating thoughtful, purposeful activities into our routines might be incredibly beneficial. Imagine scheduling 'happiness breaks' or designating certain activities as 'happiness activities' to ensure a healthy mix of both hedonic and eudemonic happiness in your day. It's a bloody good idea!

Whose happiness is it anyway?

As with everything else in life, there will be a level of external influence that plays a part in how happy we are or how we define happiness for ourselves. However, a common trap that many fall into – myself included – is mistaking someone else's version of happiness for our own. When we allow too many of these influences to alter the course of our happiness, then we're likely to be on a course to a version of success that isn't reflective of what we want in our lives, since our happiness leads to our success.

Below are a few ways that this altered trajectory can adversely affect the type and level of success that we end up achieving:

- **Loss of control.** When we let others influence our idea of success, we risk becoming dependent on others for happiness.

We can often unwittingly take advice as instruction, which is a bit like having someone else write a chapter in the book of your life, and then it stops being your book!

· **External validation.** This one crippled me for a long time. If we listen to other people's opinions too much, we forget our own opinions and eventually forget to even forge opinions in the first place. We become so focused on seeking the approval of others that we struggle to motivate ourselves and fail to stand for anything that represents us. This can lead to a paralysing dependence on others, much like the vanity metrics people chase on social media.

· **Misalignment with values.** If we lose sight of our own opinions, we run the risk of not only adopting the opinions of others but their values as well. We end up making decisions based on the framework of other people, and our own values become compromised.

· **Limiting potential.** By settling for someone else's version of happiness, we might miss out on a level of joy and fulfilment that is uniquely ours. If some of the pieces of the jigsaw belong to a different puzzle, you'll struggle to complete the picture for yourself.

All these scenarios result in a person no longer living their own life story. They become a mere shadow of their true self, leading to a deep sense of loneliness and dissatisfaction – it's not exactly a recipe for success if you can't even remember who you are!

Don't take a journey that isn't yours to take

Whether you're aware of it or not, as long as you have loved ones in your life, a portion of your happiness depends on them being happy (providing that you actually give a shit about them!).

So, for the portion of your happiness that is dependent on **you**, the question needs to be asked: how much of it is influenced by people that mean nothing to you?

Society is weird in its thoughts around being different. On a macro scale, being different is the only way to get seen these days, and that desperation to be seen is pushing people to further and further extremes. But within certain industries and cultures, particularly in Western countries, being different at any level is generally frowned upon.

I've met some amazing people in my time, and the easy observation to make is that the more genuinely individual they are (that is, they are not following the latest movement or fad), the happier they tend to be. But that's not overly easy to do these days.

Have you ever felt like the immediate community around you – whether that is professional or personal – doesn't want to see anyone do well? They seem content with the monotony of life, happy to be led by social media and the daily barrage of negativity, much like Bill Murray's character in *Groundhog Day*.

This monotonous mentality is what is commonly (and pleasantly) described as 'the comfort zone', giving people an excuse to cruise through life without ambition and without reaching a level of happiness that they could be experiencing life with. They fluff around sometimes, pretending to get things done to reach a greater level of being, but they know deep down that it's not going to happen. And worse still, they resent others for wanting to make more out of their lives.

Sound familiar? Have you been frustrated by this sort of behaviour in your world? If so, you might be stuck on what I call the Conveyor Belt of Life – the worst ride in life that nearly put me in an early grave.

Now, you can make assessments of any part of your life with this lens individually, or you can do what I did and realise that, until I was 30 if I'm being completely honest, life was happening to me rather than me being the conductor of my own life.

The first time I recognised this 'conformist' behaviour was when I was 16. All the way through school I was always pretty good with numbers and science, and so I assumed that this was the direction for me. My school encouraged this direction, as many do. It's understandable that they need to follow the societal pattern. I'm not saying that schools have an agenda, but they're designed to work students into moulds that are appropriate for the communities they are likely to be a part of.

There's an incredible TED Talk from Sir Ken Robinson called 'Do Schools Kill Creativity?' that my old mentor Rik Rushton sent to me. He encouraged me to watch it when I was at a crossroads at one stage in my career. In this talk, Robinson poses the idea that the traditional school system has a hierarchy of subjects and values science and maths over the arts (dancing, acting and so on), in accordance with what's going to be more useful for society. He also suggests that exam scores are used as tools for judgement as opposed to opportunities to find, value and nurture talent within kids.

This made me look back at my grades, and the penny dropped on an internal conflict that I had carried for years. I had a natural ability in physics and maths and gave lip service to the notion that was being pushed onto me about the prospect of university. I was never fantastic with my homework but managed to get by with half-decent grades in certain subjects that were deemed 'impressive'! Had my grades been looked at more critically, they'd have discovered a big hint as to why I do what I do in speaking, coaching and auctioneering. My maths, physics and chemistry scores were really good, but they were all eclipsed by one score – English speaking. I got a near-perfect score in that. And by some insane coincidence I find myself in a flow state when I'm onstage helping people to advance their lives in some way.

The point is this: if you feel like you're conforming to a narrative imposed by your family, community or society, explore that feeling. Ask yourself: 'If I could live **my** life, as opposed to the life I'm currently living, what would that that look like? Are there examples in the world that resemble this vision?' I'm nudging you towards the concept of living life 'by design', but I hope this will open your eyes to what **could** be possible if you follow your talents.

Of course, this isn't a call to abandon everything in your life and start afresh. There are likely aspects of your life, such as your spouse or children, that you wouldn't want to change. But the way you live your life and how you serve it has more possibilities than you might realise.

If you have a loving partner, sometimes it's a great idea to talk through these possibilities with them and either get their buy-in for whatever you have planned or get some perspective that helps you to clarify a way forward.

(PS: Don't even think about saying: 'Easy for you to say'! If you're reading this, you likely have a life that allows you to make a choice. It may be a hard choice – nothing worth having is easy – but it's still a choice!)

Chapter 12

What can you do when imposter syndrome gets in the way?

*It's not what you are that holds you back,
it's what you think you are not.*

Denis Waitley

Anyone with any level of ambition either has struggled, is currently struggling or will struggle with imposter syndrome at some point in their career or life.

The statistics around it are substantial. A 2022 KPMG study called 'Mind the gap' found that 75% of women across multiple industries suffer from imposter syndrome, and research from NerdWallet found that 78% of leaders have also struggled with it.

Despite the recognition I've earned, the respect I've received and the awareness I've gained over the years, I still ask myself: 'Do I really deserve this?' on a relatively regular basis. Writing this bloody book had me thinking about it!

Often, no matter how much effort we invest, the relentless part of our brain – the amygdala, which controls our fight-or-flight response – can activate just as we're on the brink of achieving a dream, reaching a milestone or accomplishing a goal, much like it does when we face actual danger.

When I received my award for Australian Auctioneer of the Year, I briefly felt like a king. I felt justified in my success, deserving of it and bloody proud of it too. I had worked my arse off, overcoming all of the mental health challenges, the stress of leaving the family business and everything that I had put my family through – and I felt vindicated in that moment I held the glass trophy.

Admittedly though, those feelings were short-lived. In fact, by the time I went back to my hotel after the awards night had finished up, I was already questioning whether this win meant anything. This wasn't because of the level of meaning it had for me but because of various people within my field who had questioned the validity of the award. These are still people I have a tremendous amount of respect for, who I train with and whose company I enjoy, so naturally I took their opinions on board and began to doubt the achievement I had worked so hard for over the years. Soon enough, I found myself reverting to a 'humble' version of myself, which is like toppling the first domino on a run towards irrelevance via self-deprecation and dismission of my own success.

It took me a long time to embrace the title of being number one in my chosen field, and I fear that I wasted so many opportunities off the back of effectively hiding my achievements. I suspect many of you have similar regrets, stemming from not taking full advantage of your wins when you had the chance.

For you, it might not even be about being 'the best' – it may be that you don't feel like you deserve a better life, the love of a partner or the friends that you have. It's frustrating, especially since imposter syndrome is well-documented and discussed extensively in the media, books and interviews, yet there doesn't seem to be a solution strong enough to completely eradicate it from our lives, let alone from society as a whole.

So, what can we do about it? Let's be honest, irrespective of what any brash 'entrepreneur' bleats from his social media account, imposter syndrome does not discriminate. It creates a nagging doubt within anyone striving to break free from the constraints of conformity.

Here are a few of my observations of my own struggle with imposter syndrome and how we (yes, you and me!) might navigate our way around this annoying issue that hinders so much potential from being realised.

Audit your network

Your network is the group of people you are connected to, and the strength of your network often depends on how close you are to the people within it. You have a few different networks – personal, family, work, friendship and social (both online and in person) – and they can all affect you in different ways depending on the level of importance you place on them.

Here's the thing: if you're dealing with challenges around imposter syndrome, it's likely you have some doubting voices within your networks that don't believe in who and what you are becoming and doing. A lot of the time, these voices come from people who are close to you, such as family members, loved ones or old friends from school who you've known for years. A lot of it will be well-intentioned, in that they will be cautioning you against the risk of things going wrong, but sometimes the concern can be born from a jealousy that you're trying to do something right.

Sarah Cincotta explained her experiences around this in our chat on the podcast. When Sarah launched her coaching program, she had a number of people within her professional network actively reach out to her and ask: 'Are you sure?' They doubted her ability to bring value, let alone compete with the existing coaches on the scene at the time.

Such doubts can stop plenty of great ideas in their tracks, and they very nearly stopped Sarah from following through with her program, especially since some of the doubters were people she respected. Fortunately for both her and her industry, it didn't, and she is now one of the most in-demand coaches for her niche. But she admitted that she really needed her loved ones around her for support, and she had to stop listening to certain voices within her network.

This is why it's crucial to put your networks into perspective. Rik Rushton said it best: 'If you don't value them as people, you shouldn't value their opinion'. It's essential to consider the relevance of the person to your journey before giving any weight to their opinion. I'm sure you like plenty of people, but before taking their advice to heart, consider the following:

- Do you respect the person and what they've achieved?
- Are you posing any concern or threat to them or their livelihood?
- Have they shown in the past that they have your best interests at heart?
- Have they supported you in your endeavours in the past?
- Do you trust them?

Our brains naturally act as built-in safety mechanisms – or 'bullshit radars', as they're often called – guiding us through processes like this without much thought. However, there are times when we become vulnerable to others' feedback, whether due to timing or simply because we're having a bad day. In those moments, when doubt and judgement start to creep in, it's crucial to make a more conscious effort to stay grounded.

In various areas of our lives, we may have a trusted group of people whose opinions we value. For example, you may have career mentors you wouldn't ask for dating advice from, and close mates who are great for a night out but not for financial advice! To keep things simple, I suggest typing out Rik's quote from above and keeping it handy in your phone for those times when someone's casting doubt on your thoughts and actions.

Stand guard at the gate of your mind

Any information that we receive and retain will have a conscious or subconscious influence, whether they are opinions (as mentioned earlier), (mis)information on the internet, a social media craze or the internal dialogue that kicks into gear when you're doubting your ability to handle a challenge.

Success is as much an internal game as it is external, so we need to become more mindful about the information we consume, as it all contributes to our belief in our ability to achieve success. Here are a few things I highly recommend incorporating into your way of being:

· **Monitor the quality of your thoughts.** It's easy to slip
  into negative self-talk if you're not confident in a situation
  you're in or about to be in, and when you're confronted
  by something unfamiliar. It's not entirely your fault. Our
  brains are designed to find problems, which is why we
  need to make a conscious effort to shift our thoughts when
  they turn negative. Being aware of negative thoughts and
  replacing them with positive affirmations can keep you

moving forward. You might have seen athletes look a bit silly when they spout positive self-talk, but this is what they're combating, and it doesn't look so silly when they go and achieve the ridiculous things they do!

- **Challenge negative beliefs.** Unlike temporary thoughts, negative beliefs can be deeply engrained. To rewire these beliefs into something more positive and constructive, establish a set routine or use affirmations that prime your mind more effectively. For instance, if you are constantly low on confidence when walking into work, get into the habit of telling yourself that you have the right to be confident, you are confident and you have the ability to crack on with the very best. Keep repeating it while you walk into the building, stand tall and smile as you enter your place of work. A structured routine like this can work wonders!

- **Celebrate achievements.** I've gotta admit, I'm shit at this one. I'd argue that there's not much point in setting goals if you don't celebrate in some way when you achieve them, because it takes away from the anticipation you set yourself up for when setting the goal in the first place. When you're progressing to a new level of success or a more long-term goal, it is crucial that you set progress markers and check in to see how far you've come, because you need the affirmation that your efforts have resulted in something. Otherwise, it's like trying to conquer Mount Everest in one go – not possible!

- **Seek balanced feedback.** You don't need people fluffing your ego, nor do you want anyone peeing on your bonfire constantly either! It's critical when setting forth on something that is important to you, be it a project or goal, that you identify a small number of people you **trust** to give you the good, bad and ugly feedback! It's impossible to see the whole picture while you're in the middle of it, so purposefully asking for feedback from people who you believe will bring value to your thinking is not just important, it's necessary!

- **Practise self-compassion.** Guess what? Shit is going to go wrong at some point – you'll make a mistake or say the wrong thing! You'll doubt yourself at some stage – again, it's just your brain checking in to make sure you're going in the right direction – and in those moments the last thing you want to do is not give yourself permission to process whatever negativity is kicking around inside your head. Instead of beating yourself up and compounding it, though, accept that the concern is there and give yourself a moment to let the energy settle down. It's sometimes handy to ask yourself what advice you would give to a friend if they were in the same position as you – or even better, ask a friend for their advice!

Navigating this becomes more challenging when you consider the volume of opinions and feedback our social media feeds are bombarded with, so it's important that you spend a moment to focus on how you manage this imposter syndrome – or, more accurately, your self-esteem – when navigating your social media feeds.

How much attention should you pay to opinions on social media?

It's nearly impossible not to pay **any** attention to what is thrown at you on social media, be it directly, indirectly or via the beloved algorithms. Denying that is like saying you're simply going to stick your fingers in your ears and sit in the corner with your eyes closed – you're not likely to make much progress towards success that way!

The reality is, once you put your thoughts, ideas and feelings out there, you'll probably encounter some negative feedback. Opinions are like arseholes – everyone has one, and they are entitled to have one as well. Whether it's keyboard warriors with little else going on in their lives or people who genuinely care about a topic and express a different perspective, you need to accept that you can't go through life without encountering opposing views. Comedian Ricky Gervais sums it up perfectly: 'How arrogant are you to think that you deserve to go through life with no one ever saying anything that you do not agree with or like?'

The sooner we accept that we are going to face pushback online in our pursuit of success, the quicker we can process it with reason and move on. Plus, your social feeds and followers can provide some tremendously valuable feedback that will serve you well if you have ideas or thoughts that need expanding.

Instead of being altruistic and telling you to 'switch off all of your social media', which is a massive contradiction that 'leaders' put out there (ironically on social media), let's get realistic and put some parameters in place that can help you to better navigate this social media landscape in a productive way:

- **Filter constructive and destructive feedback.** As mentioned earlier, you should really value feedback if it's coming from your trusted networks, but remember that not all feedback is relevant and useful. Let's all agree on this one: if @jantheloner68340 calls you a fucking moron with little to no reasoning as to why, then you don't need to let that affect you! If you're not sure, look at their profile to see if they're credible.
- **Prioritise key audience over critics.** As you head off on your search for success, focus on your ideal audience

(called 'avatars'). If @davethedick257 doesn't fit your key avatars and is causing a ruckus on your platform despite choosing to follow you, don't allow your trajectory to be affected by such grumpy little individuals and instead remain focused on those people who do want help, leadership, guidance or service.

- **Manage ego and criticism.** When you have a purpose, new business, mission or anything else you have a vested personal interest in, it is very easy to get defensive when it comes under scrutiny. Your ego might kick in to protect your position, but it can also limit your progress if you reject all criticism. So, if you feel your ego firing up, take a second and breathe before you react and tell whoever it is to get stuffed!

- **Stay true to your beliefs.** Ultimately, as long as you stay true to your 'North Star' – your purpose – without compromising your values, and you act in alignment with your beliefs, you won't regret your decisions. Finally, be cautious of short-term financial gains; they'll likely appear at some stage, but they shouldn't lead you astray.

If you can wrap your head around this and let it sink in, it will become something of a superpower for you. If you can take any criticism or barb online (or in person, to be fair) in the subjective way in which it's delivered, then you can hold it outside of your emotional filters and assess it pragmatically. Separating the emotion from the reality often allows you to slow down the information intake and pick out any useful stuff before you move on from it. It's something that we all wish we could do more often!

Chapter 13

What happens when the shit hits the fan?

We cannot change what we are not aware of,
and once we are aware, we cannot help but change.

Sheryl Sandberg

First, an admission! There was initially going to be a whole section of this book dedicated to mental health, the depths that I've been to with it and how that has served me to this point. However, I quickly realised that could be a whole other book. I would much rather we focus on how we can use our curiosity around success to help generate happiness for ourselves and those around us.

Yet, talking about happiness without discussing adversity, particularly in the pursuit of that elusive sense of success, is giving you only part of the picture. So, it's important to look briefly at stress, which is something that I'm guessing a lot of you have experienced or are experiencing.

Before we go on, we need to acknowledge something: life is not a journey that lets you through unscathed. We want it to be all sunshine and rainbows, and a consistent flow of dreams becoming reality, but we all know that it's somewhat different. We get challenged, pushed to the brink in various ways, and have our boundaries tested in every facet of our lives. Sometimes these challenges come all at once, and if you're already grappling with mental health issues, every other problem seems magnified. It's frustrating, to say the least. But here's the simple truth about life: the world is going to keep turning, whether you like it or not!

When I've been ill on a weekend, do you think that the agents or homeowners are really going to care? In my darkest, most desperate moments mentally, do you think a buyer was going to take it easy on me? This might sound harsh, but the reality we must face if we want to grow from our challenges is that the world doesn't really care about how we feel on any given day.

We all have responsibilities and people we are accountable for and to. We all have bills to pay, and as much as we want it to, the world isn't going to stop just because we have problems or worries. So, we need to accept that and work on what we can do to improve situations and resolve problems.

Where does stress come from?

To be honest, it's not much of a gamble to suggest that you've copped some stress in your life for whatever reason, and there is a stack of data these days to prove that you are far from being the only one. There are so many potential sources of stress that we are exposed to, more than ever when you consider the volume of media that we interact with and on.

A 2020 study conducted by the Australian Institute of Health and Welfare reported that an estimated 59% of Aussies had experienced stress in the preceding 12 months, and in 2023 the Australian Bureau of Statistics reported that 42.9% have now experienced a mental disorder of some description (which is what the initial stress causes), so it's very likely that most people around you have dealt with some kind of stress-related issue.

Understandably, the causes of stress vary depending on demographics because what is deemed important varies. In a survey by the Mental Health Foundation in the UK, for people aged between 18 and 24 the biggest cause of stress was being compared to others. More than one in five were stressed over finances, women were way more stressed than men when it came to body image, and adults over 55 stressed more about the health of a loved one. Between business pressures, relationship issues, information overload and parenting, it's easy to see why so many people get stressed out – and when you throw a problem into the mix, alarm bells may be quick to ring!

It's actually a freeing experience if you can accept that stress is going to happen in your life and problems will inevitably occur. It allows you to focus on who you are in the midst of challenging times.

What do you do when things go wrong?

One of my all-time favourite quotes, which I nearly got tattooed on myself (and still might), is often attributed to Winston Churchill: 'Success is not final, failure is not fatal. It is the courage to continue that counts'. Churchill was a man of faith, not just in God but also in his plans and strategies, which gave him the courage to continue.

This quote also makes me think that as long as there's time left in the game of life, there will still be chances to both win and lose, so we've got to keep pushing on with our purpose and be loyal to that until the final whistle of life blows.

As mentioned by Kay Bretz, an international ultramarathon runner who was a guest on the podcast, and who is both as mad as a box of frogs and tremendously composed at the same time, there are always two scenarios when we're faced with a problem: the reality and our perception of that reality, which is invariably altered by our emotions. As Kay said while describing his challenge of getting lost on one of his massive races: 'We need to separate the emotion from the situation, deal with the situation and process the emotion later when we have the time'.

During that episode, we both concluded that the key to dealing with problems is the ability to slow down time in your mind and give yourself the chance to separate the emotion from the reality.

During my own psychological work, I discovered a running order for processing a problem:

1. **Recognise the problem.** This may seem obvious, but it's surprising how many people can't do this! In fact, we all miss problems from time to time, especially if it's a problem that isn't immediately **your** problem to begin with – for example, you've forgotten to do something that your significant other had asked you to do… a few times!

2. **Acknowledge and ACCEPT the emotions.** Emotions grow if they are not addressed. Grief is one of the main culprits here, and you may well know someone who hasn't managed to process the loss of a loved one, but we all avoid facing up to emotions that aren't nice. Like a Band-Aid, though, the quicker you rip it, the less painful it is, and the quicker you accept that something's shit, the quicker you can see things more clearly.

3. **Assess the lay of the land.** Once you've allowed the wave of emotion to rush through, you can start to look at things more pragmatically. Recognise the various parts to the problem and assess what needs to be prioritised.

4. **Take the first step.** This is always the hardest one, right?
   A lot of the time, we can become overwhelmed by the scale
   of a problem, but when you're faced with a challenge, the
   worst thing you can do is nothing. So, just focus on that first
   step and take things one step at a time. And if you're not
   taking immediate action, you'd better be learning what you're
   going to need to do in advance!

How do you get better at solving problems?

The key to solving problems lies in what I said earlier: if you accept
that problems will occur, you'll be in a much better headspace to
tackle them when they do.

I found an amazing summation of how to improve your ability
to solve problems in a *Medium* article by Mat Helme, a designer.
In it, he refers to 'The Four P's to Problem Solving':

1. First, there's a need to **prepare** for what problems may occur.
   Primarily this means that we need to empower ourselves
   with as much knowledge as possible. Paramedics don't have
   time to think – they have to rely on their quick decision-
   making skills, which only improve the more they know and
   understand the subject of how to save people's lives!

2. The second P is **plan.** As I mentioned earlier in the book,
   I use visualisation strategies to play out any potential auction
   scenarios that may occur. The more you can simulate
   potential scenarios, the better you'll feel about encountering
   them should they appear. This is where many people get lazy
   and then end up chasing their tail when something happens.

3. Third, we need to **perform** – that is, to go and get shit done.

4. Finally, it's a tremendous idea to **perfect**, which means
   that by reviewing the outcomes of your attempt to fix the

problem, you can learn from any mistakes that were made, recognise what went well and have a much better idea as to how you can do better next time.

*

Happiness is an underrated superpower in my opinion. We all know how good it feels, we would all love to be happy on a more regular basis, but happiness is an undeniable energy form that lifts you as well as those around you. Finding success is way easier if you're happy, tasks and challenges don't seem as taxing, and life just feels that bit brighter, which makes finding opportunities that much easier.

It really is a critical piece in our pursuit of success; it's almost like the battery that we need to click in to make it all go. With that in mind, making it a priority is rather advisable, because you'll reach your version of success way more quickly if you do.

Final thoughts

It's safe to say that the world we live in is more confusing than ever. Everyone seems to have something to say about how you should live your bloody life. After reading my opinion on it all and seeing the stack of evidence to suggest I might be onto something, I hope you've gained a few insights that'll help you translate what you know into meaningful action.

It's important to understand that none of the four key elements – success, influence, connection and happiness – can survive or thrive without the other three. You can't be successful if you're not happy, you can't be that happy if you don't get to share that happiness with others, being influential is really difficult if you can't connect with people (or yourself), and what good does it do to connect with people if you have no idea what success looks like for you or them?

If you feel fired up after reading this book, you know what you need to do, how you need to do it and why, so crack on now that we've removed the barriers to entry and eradicated those excuses that have been like anchors holding you back in a sea of opportunities.

Where to from here?

All being well, I've helped to open your mind to the prospect that success can exist in your life to a greater extent than what you're currently experiencing. Together, we've dispelled some myths, evidenced some realities and looked at some frameworks and suggestions to help you put one foot in front of the other and head towards a vision that feels more like 'you'.

From here, the rubber needs to hit the road, and there's only one person who can make that happen. (Hint: take a look in the mirror!) How can you make those first steps towards the new horizon feel achievable? You can't tackle everything at once – that would be a recipe for disaster! However, it's crucial not to let too much time pass before taking action. If you delay, your enthusiasm might wane, and you could end up back in the same cycle as before. Like the oxygen mask in the airplane, you need to work on yourself before helping anyone else.

Start to believe in more for yourself

Note how I didn't say 'believe in yourself' but 'believe in more for yourself'. Let's start to change the narrative moving forward and believe in more than just what is within us.

First, go through the values exercise in the introduction again if you haven't already, and own the values that come out of it for you. Those things should ring true every time you look at them or say them to yourself. When you show your list to people who know you, they should be able to look at those values and say: 'Yep, that sums you up'.

This is when shit gets interesting! Give yourself permission to do one thing – dream. Throughout this book, you've learned that the limitations you've imposed on yourself, or those imposed by life, are just limitations, not unchangeable rules. I've given you enough psychological and physical evidence to show you that you absolutely can move forward in life and move to the beat of your drum and no one else's.

Avoid fantastical dreams like flying or wielding lightning – save those for after a Marvel movie. Instead, focus on envisioning an ideal scenario within your current reality that would represent a significant step up from your present situation. Describe this new reality in vivid detail, engaging all your senses to make it feel tangible and real.

After you have described it in detail, let it sink in that the world you want is the world you could have if you attach true meaning to it. The best part is that this book has shown you this potential success is actually attainable for you, provided you genuinely want it.

How does this fit into your reality?

Your well-crafted dream needs a practical approach now. This book has given you plenty of great actions to take, but there's one resource we all have limited amounts of – time.

To make your dream achievable:

1. Work out what is most practical, meaning which parts of your dream represent the low-hanging fruit that can be achieved in a relatively short space of time.
2. Work out the knowledge required.
3. Set a handful of SMART goals around one of those short-term targets.

This is where I should be telling you to be disciplined, focused and all of those wonderful ra-ra words that are used ad nauseum in business. Instead of that, I'll say one thing while you test out your new awareness: be loyal to yourself. Just for once, give yourself the right to be loyal to something that will benefit you and your existence. Have a chat to the significant other(s) in your life and explain why this is important to you, and give this one thing a go to see how the shoe of success fits.

Once you've achieved that one thing, thus proving to yourself that you are allowed a better level of success, pick another thing and see how that goes. I bet great things start to happen both internally and externally – you'll start to feel more confident, and all of a sudden life will feel slightly less challenging and slightly more exciting.

A last word

I never thought I'd be able to write a book. I've been rubber-stamped with ADHD, I struggled to write 3000 words for the final dissertation of my degree, and I've experienced almost every doubt and trial I've outlined to you throughout this book. If we're being completely honest, most people have experienced all sorts of doubt and concern, whether they're deemed a success or not.

I am going to refrain from saying that 'if I can do it, then so can you', because I've observed that hearing that makes a lot of people not want to do it! However, even if you don't gain any value from the content of this book, it can serve as a very physical reminder that none of us are bound by the limitations we convince ourselves about! I sincerely hope that the time you've invested in reading this work of mine has been rewarded with a degree of enlightenment that allows you to see your world in a different, more opportunistic light. I also hope that in reading this, you feel empowered to actually believe success is something that can exist in your world, and that success can take on the form you want it to take.

I'm going to leave you with two pearls of wisdom that my old man passed on to me, both of which you'll need when you embark upon this rather exciting part of your life.

My dad, a.k.a. 'Big Jim', was a man of few words, but also a man with a big heart. We didn't have too many meaningful father–son conversations that didn't involve sport, but we had a strong bond all the same. He was a humble guy who served his country – in the army from the age of 15 and in the police force as a detective for years – and had a knack for ballsing up DIY projects, much to my amusement and my mum's despair.

The first pearl he gave me is a great way to look at staying grounded amongst your success, which hopefully you might need in the not-too-distant future having read this book! After successfully creating a water feature in the kitchen instead of installing a wall radiator, he said: 'If you can't laugh at yourself, you shouldn't laugh at anyone else'. If you take yourself too seriously or fail to recognise your own shortcomings, then you have no right to point the finger at anyone else should they not succeed themselves.

The second pearl is simple. It's what he used to say to me before any significant event, particularly on the sports field, to let me know that he supported me: 'Get stuck in'.

The time for thinking and pontificating is over, and the time for action is now. You're ready to tackle this with energy, enthusiasm and the pride and support of those who care about you.

Thank you for being with me on this ride; I've truly appreciated your time, and I hope that it has been time well spent. I bloody well encourage you to 'get stuck in' now that I've heightened your curiosity for success. I can't wait to be influenced by your positivity as you kick on towards a level of success that you can finally be proud of.

Until next time – stay safe, stay healthy, stay happy.

Reidy

References

Chapter 1: How do we define success?

Aristotle 2009, *The Nicomachean Ethics*, tranxs. W.D. Ross, ed. Lesley Brown, Oxford University Press UK.

Holy Bible: New International Version, Proverbs 16:3.

Holy Bible: New International Version, Psalms 37:4.

Holy Bible: New International Version, Mark 8:36.

Henry Ford 1922, *Ford News*, 1 January, p. 2.

Dan White 2024, 'High Performance Humans with Dan White', *High Performance Humans*, podcast, 3 June, omny.fm/shows/high-performance-humans/high-performance-humans-with-dan-white.

Hannah Gill 2024, 'High Performance Humans with Hannah Gill', *High Performance Humans*, podcast, 5 February, omny.fm/shows/high-performance-humans/podcast10-hannah-gill.

Danielle Weber 2024, 'High Performance Humans with Danielle Weber', *High Performance Humans*, podcast, 29 January, omny.fm/shows/high-performance-humans/high-performance-humans-with-danielle-weber.

Francesca Dean 2024, 'High Performance Humans with Francesca Dean', *High Performance Humans*, podcast, 15 April, omny.fm/shows/high-performance-humans/high-performance-humans-with-francesca-dean.

American Psychological Association 2022, *Stress in America*, apa.org/news/press/releases/stress.

Dr Narelle Haworth 1998, *Fatigue and fatigue research: The Australian experience*, Accident Research Centre, monash.edu/muarc/archive/our-publications/papers/fatigue.

Seneca 2005, *On the Shortness of Life*, trans. C.D.N. Costa, Penguin Books.

Marcus Aurelius 2006, *Meditations*, trans. Martin Hammond, Penguin Books.

Elizabeth A. Kensinger 2009, 'Remembering the details: Effects of emotion', *Emotion Review*, vol. 1, no. 2, pp. 99–113.

Walter Mischel 1970, *Stanford marshmallow experiment*, en.wikipedia.org/wiki/Stanford_marshmallow_experiment.

Dr Terrie E. Moffitt et al. 2011, 'A gradient of childhood self-control predicts health, wealth, and public safety', *Proceedings of the National Academy of Sciences*, vol. 108, no. 7, pp. 2693–8, www.pnas.org/doi/10.1073/pnas.1010076108.

Chapter 2: Is setting goals the path to your success?

Stephen R. Covey 2011, *The 7 Habits of Highly Effective People*, Simon & Schuster UK.

Erik Fisher & Jim Woods 2014, *Ready Aim Fire! A practical guide to setting and achieving goals*, CreateSpace Independent Publishing Platform.

Brian Tracy 2018, *Goals! How to get everything you want – faster than you ever thought possible*, 2nd edn, Berrett-Koehler.

Gail Matthews 2007, *Goals research study*, www.dominican.edu/sites/default/files/2020-02/gailmatthews-harvard-goals-researchsummary.pdf.

Amish Aghera et al. 2018, 'A randomized trial of SMART goal enhanced debriefing after simulation to promote educational actions', *Western Journal of Emergency Medicine: Integrating Emergency Care with Population Health*, vol. 19, no. 1, pp. 112–120, pubmed.ncbi.nlm.nih.gov/29383065.

Chapter 3: How can you stay motivated?

Richard M. Ryan & Edward L. Deci 2019, *Brick by brick: The origins, development, and future of self-determination theory*, selfdeterminationtheory.org/wp-content/uploads/2019/06/2019_RyanDeci_BrickByBrick_PrePrint.pdf.

Calm.com, *How to find your passion in life in 5 mindful steps*, calm.com/blog/how-to-find-your-passion.

Dwayne Johnson (@TheRock) 2012, *Success isn't always about 'greatness'*, Twitter, 8 June.

Alan Watts 2023, *The lie we live: Alan Watts on the illusion of time*, YouTube, *True Meaning* channel, www.youtube.com/watch?v=ogLc7M9_hR8.

Eckhart Tolle 2024, *Most humans are never fully present in the now*, Instagram, 31 October.

Chapter 4: What else impacts success?

Steve Martin 1974, *Let's Get Small*, Warner Bros.

Kristy Goodwin 2024, 'High Performance Humans with Dr Kristy Goodwin', *High Performance Humans*, podcast, 29 April, omny.fm/shows/high-performance-humans/high-performance-humans-with-dr-kristy-goodwin

David Finkel 2018, 'New study shows you're wasting 21.8 hours a week', *Inc. Australia*, inc-aus.com/david-finkel/new-study-shows-youre-wasting-218-hours-a-week.html.

Helen Pluut & Jaap Wonders 2020, 'Not able to lead a healthy life when you need it the most: Dual role of lifestyle behaviors in the association of blurred work-life boundaries with well-being', *Frontiers in Psychology*, vol. 11, ncbi.nlm.nih.gov/pmc/articles/PMC7786197.

Amanda Delosa 2024, 'The importance of delivering YOUR message, in YOUR time', *High Performance Humans*, podcast, 15 July, omny.fm/shows/high-performance-humans/the-importance-of-delivering-your-message-in-your.

Sibile Marcellus 2021, 'Millennials or Gen Z: Who is doing the most job-hopping?', *Yahoo! Finance*, finance.yahoo.com/news/millennials-or-get-z-who-is-doing-the-most-job-hopping-112733374.html.

Xref 2024, *Gen Z career aspirations in Australia: Insights from Top 100 Employers Report 2024*, xref.com/blog/navigating-gen-zs-career-aspirations-in-australia.

GreenMatch 2024, *Are coffee pods and capsules bad for the environment?*, www.greenmatch.co.uk/is-coffee-pods-and-capsules-bad-for-environment.

Brian Dean 2024, 'Uber statistics: How many people ride with Uber?', Backlinko, backlinko.com/uber-users.

Dimitrije Curcic 2022, 'Self-help books statistics', WordsRated, wordsrated.com/self-help-books-statistics.

Martha Newson, Michael Buhrmester & Harvey Whitehouse 2016, 'Explaining lifelong loyalty: The role of identity fusion and self-shaping group events', *PLoS ONE*, vol. 11, no. 8, p. e0160427, ncbi.nlm.nih.gov/pmc/articles/PMC4980014.

Bernard Desmond 2024, 'When persistence meets positivity, success shines through!', *High Performance Humans*, podcast, 19 August, omny.fm/shows/high-performance-humans/when-persistence-meets-positivity-success-shines-t.

Patrick McGimpsey & Aaron Broverman 2023, 'Different types of cryptocurrencies explained', *Forbes Advisor*, www.forbes.com/advisor/au/investing/cryptocurrency/different-types-of-cryptocurrencies-explained.

Tracxn.com 2024, *Artificial Intelligence companies globally*, tracxn.com/d/sectors/artificial-intelligence/__cbMnXfS2GfFo4Vi2dxZyUy7l4O8Wyz VYLseb9keW5cI/companies.

Statista 2024, *Spending on digital transformation technologies and services worldwide from 2017 to 2027*, www.statista.com/statistics/870924/worldwide-digital-transformation-market-size.

Foundry 2023, *Digital Business Study 2023*, resources.foundryco.com/download/digital-business-executive-summary.

Peter Bendor-Samuel 2019, *Why digital transformations fail*, Everest Group, www.everestgrp.com/2019-08-why-digital-transformations-fail-3-exhausting-reasons-blog-51164.html.

Jonathan Creek 2024, 'The reasons WHY stuff goes viral!', *High Performance Humans*, podcast, 12 August, omny.fm/shows/high-performance-humans/the-reasons-why-stuff-goes-viral-jonathan-creek.

Seneca 1974, *Letters from a Stoic: Epistulae Morales Ad Lucilium*, trans. Robin Campbell, Penguin Books.

Doug Ramsey 2009, 'UC San Diego experts calculate how much information Americans consume', University of California San Diego, press release, https://library.ucsd.edu/dc/object/bb45115878/_1.pdf.

Albert Bandura 1976, 'Self-efficacy: Toward a unifying theory of behavioral change', *Psychological Review*, vol. 84, no. 2, pp. 192–215, educational-innovation.sydney.edu.au/news/pdfs/Bandura%201977.pdf

Part II: Influence

CB Insights 2023, *The first billionaire YouTuber is going after Coca-Cola and PepsiCo*, www.cbinsights.com/research/youtube-billionaire-prime-valuation.

Chapter 5: Who wants to be an 'influencer'?

Kerryn Harvey 2024, 'High Performance Humans with Kerryn Harvey', *High Performance Humans*, podcast, 25 March, omny.fm/shows/high-performance-humans/high-performance-humans-with-kerryn-harvey.

Michael H. Hart 1992, *The 100: A ranking of the most influential persons in history*, 2nd edn, Citadel Press.

Maz Farrelly 2024, 'High Performance Humans with Maz Farrelly', *High Performance Humans*, podcast, 18 March, omny.fm/shows/high-performance-humans/high-performance-humans-with-maz-farrelly-1.

Jon Levy 2021, *You're Invited: The art and science of connection, trust, and belonging*, Harper Business.

Chapter 6: How do you harness your influence?

Dale Carnegie 1936, *How to Win Friends and Influence People*, Simon & Schuster.

Tony Robbins, *How to benefit from positive thinking*, www.tonyrobbins.com/positive-thinking.

Lev Vygotsky 1987, 'Thinking and Speech', in R. W. Rieber, & A. S. Carton (eds.), *The Collected Works of L. S. Vygotsky* (Vol. 1), Plenum Press (original work published 1934).

John Antonakis, Robert J. House & D.K. Simonton 2017, 'Can super smart leaders suffer from too much of a good thing? The curvilinear effect of intelligence on perceived leadership behavior', *Journal of Applied Psychology*, vol. 102, no. 7, pp. 1003–1021, psycnet.apa.org/record/2017-14279-001.

Scott Bateman 2024, 'High Performance Humans with Scott Bateman', *High Performance Humans*, podcast, 13 May, omny.fm/shows/high-performance-humans/high-performance-humans-with-scott-bateman.

Dan White 2024, 'High Performance Humans with Dan White', *High Performance Humans*, podcast, 3 June, omny.fm/shows/high-performance-humans/high-performance-humans-with-dan-white.

Project.co 2023, *Communication statistics 2023*, www.project.co/communication-statistics-results-2023.

Stephen R. Covey 2011, *The 7 Habits of Highly Effective People*, Simon & Schuster UK.

National Literacy Trust 2024, *Children and young people's writing in 2024*, literacytrust.org.uk/research-services/research-reports/children-and-young-peoples-writing-in-2024.

Leanne Pilkington 2024, 'High Performance Humans with Leanne Pilkington', *High Performance Humans*, podcast, 8 April, omny.fm/shows/high-performance-humans/high-performance-humans-with-leanne-pilkington.

Salah Bazzi et al. 2018, *Stability and predictability in dynamically complex physical interactions*, www.ncbi.nlm.nih.gov/pmc/articles/PMC7187481.

Kendra Cherry 2023, 'What is the negativity bias?', *Verywell Mind*, www.verywellmind.com/negative-bias-4589618.

Kay Bretz 2024, 'High Performance Humans with Kay Bretz', *High Performance Humans*, podcast, 18 June, omny.fm/shows/high-performance-humans/high-performance-humans-with-kay-bretz.

Chapter 7: Why do you need an online influence?

Statista 2024, *Worldwide digital population 2024*, www.statista.com/statistics/617136/digital-population-worldwide.

Sarah Cincotta 2024, 'High Performance Humans with Sarah Cincotta', *High Performance Humans*, podcast, 6 May, omny.fm/shows/high-performance-humans/hi-performance-humans-with-sarah-cincotta.

Amanda Delosa 2024, 'The importance of delivering YOUR message, in YOUR time', *High Performance Humans*, podcast, 15 July, omny.fm/shows/high-performance-humans/the-importance-of-delivering-your-message-in-your.

Sophie Venz 2024, 'Top website statistics for 2024', *Forbes Advisor*, www.forbes.com/advisor/au/business/software/website-statistics.

Jonathan Creek 2024, 'The reasons WHY stuff goes viral!', *High Performance Humans*, podcast, 12 August, omny.fm/shows/high-performance-humans/the-reasons-why-stuff-goes-viral-jonathan-creek.

OnlineTherapy 2022, *6 in 10 Americans say social media negatively affects their mental health*, onlinetherapy.com/6-in-10-americans-say-social-media-negatively-affects-their-mental-health.

Patrick Whatman 2024, 'Analysis of 11 billion mentions: social media is more negative than ever', *Mention*, 10 July, mention.com/en/blog/social-media-mentions-analysis.

Samantha McLean 2023, 'High Performance Humans with Elite Agent's Samantha McLean', *High Performance Humans*, podcast, 20 November, omny.fm/shows/high-performance-humans/high-performance-humans-with-elite-agents-samantha.

Chapter 8: Connect with yourself before you connect with other people

Psychology Today, *Neuroplasticity*, www.psychologytoday.com/au/basics/neuroplasticity.

Timothy Ferriss 2007, *The 4-Hour Work Week*, The Crown Publishing Group.

Matthew Thorpe & Rachael Ajmera 2024, 'How meditation benefits your mind and body', Healthline, www.healthline.com/nutrition/12-benefits-of-meditation#stress.

Mental Health Foundation, *How to look after your mental health using exercise*, www.mentalhealth.org.uk/explore-mental-health/publications/how-look-after-your-mental-health-using-exercise.

Tim Blankert & Melvyn R.W. Hamstra 2017, 'Imagining success: Multiple achievement goals and the effectiveness of imagery', *Basic and Applied Social Psychology*, vol. 39, no. 1, pp. 60–67, www.ncbi.nlm.nih.gov/pmc/articles/PMC5351796.

Australian Bureau of Statistics 2023, *National Study of Mental Health and Wellbeing*, www.abs.gov.au/statistics/health/mental-health/national-study-mental-health-and-wellbeing/latest-release.

Katherine R. Arlinghaus & Craig A. Johnston 2019, 'The importance of creating habits and routine', *American Journal of Lifestyle Medicine*, vol. 12, no. 2, pp. 142–144, www.ncbi.nlm.nih.gov/pmc/articles/PMC6378489.

Simon Sinek 2011, *Start With Why*, Penguin Books.

Janice Omadeke 2022, 'The best leaders aren't afraid to be vulnerable', *Harvard Business Review*, 23 July, hbr.org/2022/07/the-best-leaders-arent-afraid-of-being-vulnerable.

Ethan Kross et al. 2014, 'Self-talk as a regulatory mechanism: How you do it matters', *Journal of Personality and Social Psychology*, vol. 106, no. 2, pp. 304–324, selfcontrol.psych.lsa.umich.edu/wp-content/uploads/2014/01/KrossJ_Pers_Soc_Psychol2014Self-talk_as_a_regulatory_mechanism_How_you_do_it_matters.pdf.

James Clear 2018, *Atomic Habits*, Avery Publishing Group.

Chapter 9: How do you connect one-on-one?

T. Franklin Murphy 2022, 'Activity Theory', *Psychology Fanatic*, 2 August, psychologyfanatic.com/activity-theory.

Tree Meinch 2022, 'We're beginning to understand the power of eye contact', *Discover*, discovermagazine.com/mind/were-beginning-to-understand-the-power-of-eye-contact.

John M. Gottman & Joan DeClaire 2001, *The Relationship Cure: A 5 step guide to strengthening your marriage, family, and friendships*, Three Rivers Press.

Chapter 10: How do you win over a crowd and connect at scale?

Immy Callister 2023, 'High Performance Humans with Immy Callister', *High Performance Humans*, podcast, 4 December, omny.fm/shows/high-performance-humans/high-performance-humans-with-immy-callister.

Oana Aurora 2017, '5 steps to reveal your personal USP', *Medium*, medium.com/@oanaaurora/5-steps-to-reveal-your-personal-usp-a8ee3d18b836.

Part IV: Happiness

Jayne W. Barnard 2008, 'Narcissism, over-optimism, fear, anger, and depression: The interior lives of corporate leaders', *University of Cincinnati Law Review*, papers.ssrn.com/sol3/papers.cfm?abstract_id=1136888.

Paul B. Lester et al. 2021, 'Happy soldiers are highest performers', *Journal of Happiness Studies*, vol. 23, pp. 1099–1120, ppc.sas.upenn.edu/sites/default/files/happysoldiershighperformers.pdf.

Chapter 11: What defines happiness for you?

Robert Waldinger (study director), *Harvard Study of Adult Development*, www.adultdevelopmentstudy.org.

Chris Helder 2023, 'High Performance Humans with Chris Helder', *High Performance Humans*, podcast, 27 November, omny.fm/shows/high-performance-humans/high-performance-humans-with-chris-helder.

Sir Ken Robinson 2006, *Do schools kill creativity?*, www.ted.com/talks/sir_ken_robinson_do_schools_kill_creativity?

Chapter 12: What can you do when imposter syndrome gets in the way?

KPMG International 2022, *Mind the Gap*, assets.kpmg.com/content/dam/kpmg/xx/pdf/2022/12/mind-the-gap.pdf.

Connor Campbell 2022, 'Over three quarters of UK business leaders have experienced impostor syndrome', *NerdWallet*, 13 December, www.nerdwallet.com/uk/business/imposter-syndrome.

Sarah Cincotta 2024, 'High Performance Humans with Sarah Cincotta', *High Performance Humans*, podcast, 6 May, omny.fm/shows/high-performance-humans/hi-performance-humans-with-sarah-cincotta.

Chapter 13: What happens when the shit hits the fan?

Australian Institute of Health and Welfare 2024, *Stress and trauma*, aihw.gov.au/reports/mental-health/stress-and-trauma.

Australian Bureau of Statistics 2020–2022, *National Study of Mental Health and Wellbeing*, abs.gov.au/statistics/health/mental-health/national-study-mental-health-and-wellbeing/2020-2022.

Mental Health Foundation 2018, *Stress: statistics*, www.mentalhealth.org.uk/explore-mental-health/statistics/stress-statistics.

Kay Bretz 2024, 'High Performance Humans with Kay Bretz', *High Performance Humans*, podcast, 18 June, omny.fm/shows/high-performance-humans/high-performance-humans-with-kay-bretz.

Mat Helme 2014, 'The four P's to problem solving', *Medium*, medium.com/@MatHelme/the-four-ps-of-problem-solving-6e15a39a0712.